One Size Fits Few

The Folly of Educational Standards

Susan Ohanian

Heinemann
Portsmouth, NH

Heinemann

A division of Reed Elsevier Inc.
361 Hanover Street
Portsmouth, NH 03801–3912

Offices and agents throughout the world
http://www.heinemann.com

We would like to thank those who have given their permission to include material in this book.

Library of Congress Cataloging-in-Publication Data

Ohanian, Susan.
     One size fits few: the folly of educational standards / Susan
Ohanian.
          p.   cm.
     Includes bibliographical references and index.
     ISBN 0-325-00158-8
     1. Education—Standards—United States.   2. Education—Social
aspects—United States.   3. Education and state—United States.
I. Title.
LB3060.83.053   1999
379.1'58'0973—dc21   98-54482
                                                                CIP

Editor: Lois Bridges
Cover design: Barbara Werden
Manufacturing: Louise Richardson

Printed in the United States of America on acid-free paper
02   01   DA   5   6

For Bob Boynton, who knows a bad idea when he spots it,
who possesses a fine eye for distinguishing chalk from cheese, and
who was right when he warned me not to return to California.
Mostly for the fact that he is a fine fellow.

Contents

Introduction

Recently, I carried my Compaq notebook computer and my Canon printer on a trip to Dallas, Sacramento, and Albuquerque. Every place I stopped I bought another pack of paper, found an electrical outlet, and feverishly printed out more minutes of the meetings of various groups given a charge by the California State Board of Education to come up with standards by which teachers and students should lead their lives.

As it happens, there have been a lot of meetings, and my little printer was definitely burning the midnight oil. Back in the quietude of Vermont, it printed one letter to my parents and died. Without even a gasp of complaint, it just stopped. Dead. Clearly, I'm not overstating the case to say that my Canon printer is an early victim of the California standards overkill.

I mention the brand of my late printer not because I'm trying to emulate those pretentious, brand-name Hollywood movies, but because I'm trying to save my critics the trouble of writing the publisher and questioning my veracity. Over the years I have developed a kind of affection for hate mail, but everybody knows what sensitive souls publishers are.

Back in 1987, factophiles devoted to endless lists of minutia kids need to know wrote denunciatory letters to *Education Week*, claiming I was both a liar and a fraud because, in my energetic review of E.D. Hirsch, Jr.'s *Cultural Literacy: What Every American Needs To Know* (Houghton Mifflin, 1987) in those same pages, I'd made two impossible claims. First, I said that in just one week of owning the book I'd "worn it to shreds with my frantic flipping back and forth in the list, searching in vain for content, for consistency, for balance."

Funny thing: I gave plenty of documentation for this claim. While reading the book, I happened to be traveling, and so I:

> amazed and alarmed strangers on airplanes, in hospital waiting rooms, and in hotel lobbies by reading them portions of the list: What do you know about Leyden jars and when did you know it? How are your Mach numbers? Is your amicus curiae in working order? I have pestered colleagues in the office and called friends and relatives long distance, quizzing them about "hardwired," "biochemical pathways," and "liver detoxification"—all items on Hirsch's loony list of items students should know by the time they graduate from high school.
>
> Mr. Hirsch's avowed mission is to save public education by testing students at three stages during their school careers to ensure that they do not leave high school without the ability to recognize such terms as covalent bonds, the Edict of Nantes, non compos mentis, Planck's constant, the Slough of Despond, and scrotum.

Hey, as the daughter of an undertaker, the recipient of an MA in medieval literature, and the wife of a physicist, I know these things. But does that mean our schools should teach such esoterica?

Anybody who sets himself up as the savior of culture and literacy is, of course, on the side of the angels. Who will argue against our youth knowing Sophocles? Shakespeare? Tom Sawyer? Every teacher has experienced that vague disquiet that our students don't know as much as we'd like them to: They don't have that common corpus of nursery rhymes, fairy tales, and Bible stories we remember from our own youth. When I remarked at a family gathering that I couldn't figure out why Hirsch would posit "La Cucaracha" as necessary knowledge for a literate person, three generations of relatives broke into song.

And that is a real problem with literacy list determinists and other Standardistos. People reading the lists figure if they know the items, well then the list must be pretty good. But it is both impossible and wrong for a teacher to posit her curriculum on her generation's cultural baggage. Ecclesiastes (and Mr. Hirsch) is wrong: There are plenty of new things under the sun. And we can't keep making the lists of necessary knowledge longer and longer. Something has to go. Maybe even "La Cucaracha."

While confessing that I could join my relatives in singing "La Cucaracha," I could, if I were either desperate or daft enough, also launch into "One Meatball," "Willie the Weeper," "St. James Infirmary," and "Abdul el Bulbul Amir." My father sang me to sleep every night of my childhood, and, despite my mother's protests about "suitability for young ears," we had our cultural favorites.

The Standardisto who accused me of lying in the pages of *Education Week* also objected to this paragraph:

> I would like to announce that I do know about "throw weight," but the knowledge came at a high cost—ten minutes of waiting long distance for my husband to stop laughing and give me a lecture on naval engineering.

The Standardisto insisted that I must be lying, that nobody would waste ten minutes of long distance phone charges to listen to her husband laugh. For me, more than ten years later, this is still one of those crystal moments that reveals the world: Standardistos, not content with cleaning their own desk drawers, are confident that they can regulate the way the rest of us lead our lives, down to the length and content of our phone calls.

It just so happens that at the time of that phone call I had a job and an apartment in the Philadelphia suburbs while my husband was home with the cats hundreds of miles away. So phone laughter was as close as I could get to the real thing. Maybe it's because my students are my only estate, but I bleed over eduational insanity wherever it occurs. I knew then as I know now that it is my moral duty to offer a counterargument to people who would try to streamline, sanitize, and standardize education.

Alas, I must confess, at some point in the ensuing decade, I have lost the meaning of throw weight. It undoubtedly lies rotting in my mental graveyard of discarded facts, lying, no doubt, next to the schwa.

A few years ago, an editor cut an anecdote I'd written about schwas on the grounds it was an "obvious exaggeration" (editorialese for "a lie"). "Nobody," he insisted, "would believe that an experienced reading teacher doesn't know what a schwa is." That's the Standardisto psyche speaking: Standardistos are confident in their assertions of what everybody else should know. Some people just figure that it's easier to call me a liar than to face the education truths I describe: In the grand scheme of things, throw weights and schwas just don't count for much.

I used to mention my schwa deficit in speeches, but then I had to deal with all the earnest reading teachers who afterwards insisted on telling me. All I can say is that my deliberate and continued ignorance of schwas seems to be an important feature of my psychological well-being. I've known plenty of students just as stubborn, and when that obdurate hard-headedness sets in, I know to move on to more important matters.

Although E.D. Hirsch is opposed to national or even state standards, believing that every school should make its own curriculum decisions, his endlessly proliferating lists of facts every school kid needs to know are at the heart of many Standardisto factoid-crammed documents. Give a Standardisto a pad of paper and a pencil and he goes nuts making lists of essential knowledge—without ever laying eyes on the children who must learn it. Intellectually, I get a good chuckle at the bizarre idea that I should teach the Edict of Nantes, non compos mentis, Planck's constant, the Slough of Despond, and scrotum to my students. But when we get down to the realities of classrooms, the realities of the individual children in our care, the antics of Standardistos are no longer funny. We need not wonder what alien power has taken over the collective cerebrums of Standardistos; what we need to do is fight back.

In the name of quality, the Standardistos offer a curriculum of death to children not already on the advanced placement track to elite universities. To do what educators too often do—sit back and say, "This too will pass," is to condemn hundreds of thousands of students to the academic refuse bin. Our policy makers and politicians are pretending that every third grader will read on grade level simply because the chief Standardisto, the President, has issued a proclamation. In New York, politicians proclaim no high schooler will get a diploma without passing regents exams; in Chicago, bureaucrats proclaim no kid will get out of fourth grade until he passes the reading test. We need a reality check. Are they going to build special places for all the high school dropouts? Special schools for the sixteen-year-olds in fourth grade? Haven't the Standardistos ever met the recalcitrant kids who don't toe the line? Who don't do homework? Or the kids who, despite all best efforts, don't progress according to a timetable devised at some publishing conglommerate? Haven't they met kids who can recite their consonant blends in their sleep but still can't read? What will these standards do to these kids?

One-third of the students who enter ninth grade in California do not graduate four years later. And so the California State Board of Education, in its wisdom, has passed a set of standards that seems intent on killing the kids off before they reach ninth grade: According to one of eleven history standards in seventh grade, students must analyze the geographic, political, economic, religious, and social structures of the civilizations of Islam and China in the Middle Ages.

This book offers a challenge to such insanity.

My dead-from-exhaustion printer was a Canon BJ-10. Viewing hours are available by appointment.

1

Whose Standards These Are, I Think I Know

THAT'S NOT A KID, THAT'S A SCOPE-AND-SEQUENCE CHART

*T*o the Standardistos who don't know kids but do know products, I commend a Kurt Vonnegut story where a young man admiring the centerfold of a girlie magazine, says, "Look at that woman!" The older man replies, "Son, that's not a woman, that's a photograph." I'd say the same to Standardistos who rely on skills charts and standardized test scores for their notion of children. I want to tell them, "People, those aren't children, those are numbers."

Members of the media have a singular inability to look beyond the charts and see real children. When an editor at *USA Today* phoned, asking me to write an op–ed piece about Goals 2000, President Clinton's refried Bush plan for national standards and measures, I was elated at the idea of being able to show the difficulties these standards present to children and their teachers. As I'd done often in the past, I wrote a poignant little 800-word piece for *USA Today*. In the past, the *USA Today* editorial team had expressed enthusiasm for my writing, publishing my columns without changing a word. This time, I expressed concern that a standardized curriculum gives nonstandard students no place to go. I described the way Jack remade himself in our storefront high school—set up for kids too obnoxious to be allowed on the regular campus. Jack didn't learn quadratic equations; he didn't read *Hamlet*. But while studying his self-chosen subject of Scrabble four hours a day for six months, he began to acquire the tools he needed to change the destructive course of his life. This boy was so obnoxious that his mother kicked him out and in the middle of winter, and when he couldn't find a car to sleep in, he broke into our school. Jack's beginning curriculum with us was:

1) Do not utter profanities;

2) Read half an hour.

Jack was allowed to study Scrabble as long as he curbed his filthy tongue and didn't pester other students beyond endurance. I use the word "study" quite deliberately. I started the whole business by showing Jack an article from *Harpers* about street hustlers who made a living playing Scrabble. Then Jack pestered me until I bought him the dictionary mentioned in the article, a dictionary heavy on word roots. Jack sat in a corner, studied the dictionary, and played against himself.

And he read half an hour a day. I took Jack on a scouting raid for used paperbacks and Dick Francis and Zane Grey emerged as his favorites. Jack said he'd read more in one month at our school than he'd read in the previous ten years combined. After six months of Scrabble immersion, Jack began working his way through our teacher-created curriculum; he completed graduation requirements in two years. Then came my moral test: Although commending someone I cared about to the Marine Corps stretched my personal standards to the limit, Jack helped me see that this was a good course for him. That's what school should be about: Teachers and curriculum being flexible enough to meet the needs of each student, not shoving every kid through some distant committee's phantasmic pipe dream of a necessary curriculum for tomorrow's workforce.

The *USA Today* editor told me Jack's story was all fine and good—but far too "unique" for their readers. And so I wrote another piece, describing another nonstandard student. And another. And another. With each piece I made the plea for schools that acknowledge and nurture students' different strengths, schools able to come up with oddball plans for oddball students. Through my anecdotes about quite wonderful students, I tried to show why the Standardisto plan to abandon students, refusing them a high school diploma if they fail to pass a test on quadratic equations, is insane. Standardistos ignore the fact that we need our students to grow up to become chefs, plumbers, child-care workers, musicians, and poets as well as engineers and certified public accountants. Most important, we need our students to grow up to become parents who nurture their children. Our nation of school teachers must not accept the Standardistos' one-size-fits-all curriculum plan. A teacher's individual curriculum choices become increasingly vital as our society devalues its children. As nurturers in classrooms across America, we must care more about how often our graduates read to their children than whether they have deconstructed *The Scarlet Letter* or *Tale of Two Cities*.

The people designing ideal curriculum standards have the notion that knowledge is pure, and unrelated to the knowledge seeker. This, of course, is nonsense. We cannot offer a curriculum without considering the students. For starters, the number of children in foster or residential care hit 462,000 in 1994. That's nearly double the figure of 1985. To add a double whammy, a high percentage of these kids are being schooled in substandard buildings where the roof leaks and where officials can't find enough teachers to cover the classes.

All this talk of individual, oddball students stretched the patience of the *USA Today* editor. He wanted to talk about numbers that go bump in the night, about how the kids in Grosse Pointe measure up against the kids in Larchmont or Palo Alto and how both compare to the Japanese. Anecdotes about oddball urban kids aren't on this military-industrial-infotainment complex agenda. This agenda, pushed by the Standardistos, insists that we can know our students by their number 2 pencil numbers. They brook no talk about the ambiguity of the schoolhouse. Standardisto documents delineate teaching and learning as a neat and tidy thing. I object. By turning pedagogy into narrative, I hope to address the messiness of the teaching-learning compact.

Standardistos turn a deaf ear to our stories because without these stories we are invisible. And without our stories our students are invisible, too. Invisible and voiceless. Students, lacking a vote and lacking the lobbyists to put $30 million into the pockets of Congress and billions into newspaper advertising the way tobacco interests did, are invisible to politicians and newspaper editors. We teachers are pretty much invisible, too, but the very least we can do is tell the children's stories.

What the *USA Today* editor really wanted me to write about is kids like his, kids like the sons and daughters of the businessmen sitting at breakfast reading the free copies of *USA Today* the hotel provides. These are the people who want our classrooms to be more like the classrooms of the Japanese and less like the classroom I provided for Jack. Of course, anyone who knows schools knows that Jack's case is not unique. Edward Silver, senior scientist, Learning Research Development Center, University of Pittsburgh, talks passionately about a student he encountered early in his career, a South Bronx boy who might have been Jack's cousin, a boy who spent most of the seventh grade pursuing his obsession with numerical palindromes. Speaking at the 1998 National Convocation on Mathematics Education in the Middle Grades, held at the National Academy of Sciences in Washington, D.C., Silver dryly observed, "You can learn a lot of algebra by studying palindromes." Look in vain at the California mathematics standards, discussed in Chapter Five, for any mention of numerical palindromes. Look at any state standards. When teachers write textbooks that try to show students that algebra need not be as dry as dust, the *Wall Street Journal*, among others, runs a front-page story about "fuzzy math." Nonetheless, teachers must persist; they must be ever alert to the needs of one seventh grader, helping that child to see the value of whimsy and wonder—and honoring his idiosyncratic obsession—in a knowledge-building plan for the day. That's all we can hope for: Doing good today.

WHO BENEFITS FROM MORE TESTS?

I asked the *USA Today* editor, "Oh, you want me to write about the regular kids, the kids who are reading on grade level already?" I agreed that I could do that, but I asked him, "What's the point?" Since every teacher and every parent in the country already knows which kids are performing on grade level and which ones aren't, who benefits from new, national tests besides the people selling them? Students already take from four to eight standardized tests a year. What the education world needs is a few strong administrators and teachers and parents to join together, proclaiming, "Enough is enough"—people who know how to say "We're as mad as hell, and we're not going to do this any more."

Every time I'd e-mail a story about another of my students as proof positive that schools need to broaden curriculum options rather than stiffen traditional requirements, an argument ensued. The affable *USA Today* editor admitted he knows his own child's reading and math scores; he even admitted that he's satisfied with those scores and is well-satisfied with his child's school. "I know my daughter's teacher is excellent," he said, adding, "I know you're probably an excellent teacher, too, but we need high standards to raise up all those teachers out there who aren't excellent."

This is the tactic made infamous by Joseph McCarthy. Point to the unnamed dastardly creatures who are bringing the country to the brink of disaster. In the old days we were going to make the country safe for democracy by instituting loyalty oaths. These days, we'll do it by testing kids and testing their teachers, too. And states like California are also instituting loyalty oaths, making inservice providers promise not to talk about teaching methods not pre-approved by the Board of Education.

The *USA Today* editor seemed to be operating on a mirage theory of education. This fellow sitting in the Virginia suburbs is telling me that poor kids in crumbling urban schools will have equal opportunity for a quality education if we institute national tests and tell kids they can't graduate if they don't master quadratic equations.

By the time I sent my *piece de resistance*, a story nobody could resist, long arguments about standards had made both the editor and me giddy. But I insisted on this one last "proof" that the measure of a classroom lies outside Standardisto edicts.

A few years ago I was wandering around the Boston Book Fair on a Saturday morning when a big black man came up to me, handed me his business card, and invited me to dinner. This was a man who'd been my student in the green days of my second year of teaching. I remember Leon as the obstreperous eighth grader who, in an exceptional commentary on textbook standards when his teacher was absent and an ineffectual substitute in charge, led a pack of his peers in dumping all the social studies texts out of the third floor window into the snow below. I also remember him as the kid who sat in the front row when we went to hear the Albany symphony, pulling out his harmonica and playing along. Leon says he remembers me as the teacher who taught him to love books.

Maybe you have to be a teacher to realize the magic of meeting a former student at the Boston Book Fair. *USA Today* didn't see any magic. The editorial panel rejected this as just one more story about one more kid. "Not universal enough," they told me. "Not significant, not proof of teacher professionalism or standards." What? Are they nuts? Don't they recognize a miracle even when its glittering crystals cascade around them? I began to feel desperate. What did these media thugs want? That I slit my veins and bleed for them? But I resort to histrionics. I confess I knew from the first rejection what they wanted: These suburban editors don't give a damn about kids in

Chicago or Los Angeles inner-city schools. They want me to demonstrate my teacherly professionalism by calling for a nationwide test that will rank their children's ritzy schools with the ritzy schools in other rich suburbs. When I say I will bask forevermore in the glow of being the kind of teacher whose student grows up to be the kind of man who spends a Saturday morning at the Boston Book Fair, they say, "Frankly, my dear, we don't give a damn." They don't give a damn because, operating from a position of power, they don't have to.

Since talking about kids didn't work for the editorial committee at *USA Today*, I decided to demonstrate my cosmopolitanism by expounding on my research on schools in Japan. While there, I asked one question in as many ways as I could think to phrase it. I asked students, teachers, members of the Tokyo Board of Education, principals, head of the PTA, a Buddhist monk, TDK executives, a TV cameraman, a newspaper reporter, "What happens when a child fails to keep up with his peers?" Again and again I was assured this never happens. In Japan, the group of forty children who start school together stay together through sixth grade. And, by definition, they all keep pace, a standard pace, if you will.

So then I asked, "Where does that woman weeding the median strip along the highway fit into the educational and social system? How does the clerk at Maku-donarudo (McDonald's) fit into the carefully laid out educational plan that leaves nothing to chance?" I never got an answer. It was, of course, a rude question. Funny thing: Japanese officials don't want to say anything bad about their schools; our officials don't want to say anything good about ours.

I forget why the Japan piece didn't work for *USA Today*. In any case, having submitted the stories of five nonstandard students who would be hurt by national standards, having argued for hours with the editor, I cried "uncle." This was extremely hard for me to do. I pride myself on never giving up. Never. In better days, I'd written half a dozen or more op-ed pieces for *USA Today*, controversial pieces that zipped past the editorial committee scrutiny without a murmur. But when it comes to standards, obviously, I do not speak the language of the military-industrial-infotainment complex. And I'm unwilling to learn it. Of course, the editors are also unwilling to learn my language. We talk past each other—my stories are too messy; their four-color graphs are too tidy.

This story does have a moral, and the moral is this: If a teacher can't win, at least she doesn't have to roll over and play dead. She can stand up tall and look for a chance to squeal on the bastards.

PASSING A TEST

The summer when I was four years old, I passed the biggest test of my life. Dad parked our coupe on one of two main streets in our tiny town. Then he gave me instructions, "Your mother and I are going into that building. Your mother will be out very soon. Do not get out of the car until she comes back. Do you understand? *No matter what, do not get out of the car.*"

Almost as soon as they disappeared into the building, smoke wafted up from under the passenger seat. First smoke, then flames. I moved over to the driver's seat. The flames got bigger.

When my mother came out of the building, the passenger compartment was in flames, and I was crouched up on the narrow platform above the seats. She pulled me out of the car, screaming, "My God! Why didn't you get out of the car?"

I looked at her very solemnly and replied, "Daddy said, 'Don't get out, no matter what.'" I thought it was a test. I was proud I had passed.

My father, of course, was very shaken. He explained to me that he'd done a terrible thing, that nobody should ever say "never." He explained, "You can't say 'never' and you can't say 'always,' because there are exceptions."

My nine-year-old sister was very impressed. "Weren't you scared?" she asked. I smiled. She was older, every day demonstrating her ability to do so many things I couldn't do. But I was the one who had passed the test. And it was *the* test. I grew up knowing that not even my MA committee at UC Berkeley, who worked hard at cunning contrivance, could devise such a test.

Today, as I stand back from the story and try to see that small child, I am struck by the enormous vulnerability of all children. Children trust adults. Children believe what adults tell them and will quite literally suffer flames at those adults' bidding. I carried from that incident the knowledge that adults, even the ones you love, can be wrong. For me, my father was Robin Hood, Abe Lincoln, and Roy Rogers all rolled into one. After all, I grew up with the story of the day he killed thirty-six rattlesnakes. So the lesson he taught me stuck. But what also sticks, and it is the much scarier part, is the stubborn resolution of a four-year-old who would rather burn than waver.

I wish that the Standardistos could grasp the enormity of this point. I wish that Standardistos were themselves readers. Novelists, short story writers, memoirists, and, of course, poets, who prefer passion over pedagogy, elucidate this issue. In *Free Agents*, Max Apple describes stubborn, single-minded children, children who inspire awe as well as terror in their determination to martyr themselves to a principle. Max Apple's children inform us better than the Standardisto paper piles stretching to the moon and back. Apple reminds us that we adults must both recognize and honor children's best selves, and at the same time we need be ever alert and able to protect children from those best selves.

As I watch the antics of the Standardisto vigilante posses hogtieing and burning their peculiar brand onto diversity, I think of my four-year-old self, the ten-year-old Max Apple of "Stranger at the Table," and his nine-year-old daughter of "Bridging." At best, the Standardisto documents littering the land are irrelevant to the lives of children. At worst, they offer obscenity, poisoning public perception of what schools need to do. Standardistos offer a viciousness that must be laid bare. With Standardistos storming the media ramparts, teachers cannot maintain their preferred role of closing their doors and keeping quiet.

JUST SAY "NO!" TO THE TEACHER AS TECHNICIAN

John Goodlad has pointed out that every school has a curriculum, but everybody perceives this curriculum differently. This was brought home to me the first year I team-taught language arts in a newly-established program for seventh and eighth graders who tested at the bottom of standardized tests. Our class was called Language Arts Tutorial and was abbreviated LAT on the computerized report cards. We all called it LAT.

At parent conferences in the spring one mother remarked that she was happy her daughter was doing so well in our class, adding that it was the first time the girl had liked school since first grade. "I do have one question, though," confessed Mom. "I wonder why a child who had always had so much trouble with reading is taking Latin."

This wasn't just a case of Mom misunderstanding the acronym on the report card. My partner and I polled our students. Twenty-six percent thought they were taking Latin. Kids are traditionalists. As that masterful teacher and commentator Jim Herndon pointed out decades ago, kids know how things are 'spozed to be in school. My students didn't know how Latin was 'spozed to be, but they sure knew about Language Arts and Remedial Reading. My teaching partner and I prided ourselves on designing a class that broke the corrosive mold of traditional English classes. And our students, not seeing much they recognized, put two and two together and came up with Latin.

If I had a nickle for every kid who, liking my unconventional classrooms, said, "Geez, Mrs. O, I wish you was a real teacher," by now I could probably buy a couple of latte grandes. And it would just about equal the number of kids who complained that I didn't do things the way last year's teacher did them. I always held my tongue, not admitting that I'd rather be locked up in a room with only *Gulliver's Travels* as a companion than even wash the boards the way their last teacher did.

I've said it plenty of times before, and I will say it again: The really scary thing about teaching is that we teachers, particularly those of us in elementary school, teach who we are. We are the curriculum. Every story I've told for the past twenty years speaks to this point, and here's another one. One frigid winter morning Jenny realized she'd forgotten the house key she usually wore around her neck. A very responsible third grader, Jenny used her key to let herself into the apartment she shared with her single mother. Jenny left school at three PM, got home by 3:10, and immediately phoned her mother at work. Her mother then phoned back at four, just to check, and got home by five. They depended on each other to keep these schedules, and Jenny was very aware of her responsibilities in the partnership. "She already took off work this month," wailed Jenny. "She can't do it again."

Earlier in the month, when evidence of Jenny's chicken pox had erupted one morning, she was so reluctant for her mother to miss any work that I had to bodily pick up this child whose fever was palpable and carry her to the nurse. Feverish and obviously miserable, she continued to insist that she was "okay."

On the morning she discovered her key was missing, I assured Jenny, "Don't worry. We'll figure something out. But first, why don't you go down to the office and phone your mom? She will probably have a plan. Tell her I can take you somewhere or we can stay at school together until she gets off work."

Jenny came back grinning. "Mom asked my aunt to come get me."

I commented, "Your mom is terrific," as I steered her toward making her silent reading choice for the day. The next morning the first thing Jenny said was, "My mom said, 'Thank you.' "

"What?"

Jenny grinned a huge grin, "She says thank you for saying she's terrific."

Oh my God. I still get chills when I remember that moment. My remark to Jenny was one of those offhand transitional statements that fill a teacher's day, statements to lead children back into the classroom business at hand. I've long wondered why there aren't piles of learned dissertations on the words and gestures of transition; I suspect they reveal the key to a classroom culture, maybe even getting at the heart of what it means to be a teacher.

I still get chills when I think about this incident because although on that particular day I behaved well, I know I could have behaved badly: I could have shown Jenny I was busy and feeling frazzled by her carelessness with a key. I could have sent her down to deal with the office secretary on her own—without a conciliatory note—leaving her to deal on her own with the prohibition against students using the phone. I could have just said, "Time to get to work!" when she returned from the office.

I'm a good third grade teacher not because I have a master's degree in medieval literature from the University of California or a zillion course hours from New York University on teaching the humanities, but because I like kids. Plain and simple, I like them. Newspaper and TV editors are enamored by the very idea of retired military men and corporate middle managers going into the schools to teach discipline and mathematics. Well good for them for making the effort, but if they are to persevere and even triumph, then their preeminent concern must be to cherish the children in their care. We need people in our classrooms who are able to see that the parents of their students are terrific because they support their children with strength, resilience, and love—"even if" they are unmarried, have friends who sleep over, and need food stamps to make ends meet. If the retired corporate and military honchos who currently enamor the media can do this, I'm willing to let them teach math. Then, when competence fails them, love can take over.

Whenever I tell Jenny's story to teachers, I don't have to explain the significances. I wouldn't dream of trying such a story on a media type. Teachers appreciate the small anecdote both because we know our own vulnerability and because we so rarely have the leisure time to articulate our classroom practices, to voice our fears, brag about our accomplishments, share our dreams. Bureaucrats demand action plans, goal statements, and other grand gobbledygook. Nobody gives us a chance to talk about what happened yesterday.

Donald Schon calls such musings "reflection-in-action." In his review of research at the Massachusetts Institute of Technology, Schon learned that reflection-in-action is not dependent on previously-established categories of theory and technique, but "constructs a new theory of the unique case." This is exactly what the editor at *USA Today* did not want to hear from me. He wanted established categories agreed upon by some blue-ribbon commission made up of three governors, eight corporate vice-presidents, three parents with a vendetta. And a partridge in a pear tree. I persist in offering unique cases because unique cases are the only way I am willing to talk about teaching.

Schon cautions of the dangers of practitioners getting locked into a view of themselves as technical experts. When skill at technique and situational control predominate, admitting uncertainty is a sign of weakness. Security is three checks on the board, seven steps in the lesson, 178 state-issued competencies to get out of kindergarten. All I can say is that when you are strong enough to admit weakness, children will reassure and reward you. One day I yelled, "Shut up!" at Jenny's class, definitely a clamorous crew. I yelled and then I apologized immediately, blinking back a couple of tears. The children turned my vulnerability into another one of those great classroom moments. They rushed to comfort me, hugging and patting and offering testimony that my yelling was definitely not world-class. They named teachers who were world-class screamers. Leslie, the deaf child in public school for the first time, the child to whom I gave so much of my heart and about whom I've written so much, gave me a big hug and said, "Don't you worry, Mrs. O, we're going to get it. You are a good teacher, and we are going to learn it."

In the Fall of 1998, primary-grade math specialists and math professors attending an Exxon Education Foundation conference were astounded when the lecturer, noted University of Alabama Professor Constance Kamii, responded to a teacher's question about how to teach a fourth grader a particular procedure by admitting, "I have no idea." During the coffee break, the room was buzzing over this response; we talked about how unique it is in education for experts to admit they don't know something. Will the Standardisto who has ever admitted, "I have no idea," please make herself known?

CHASING GROUNDHOGS AND OTHER PILLAGERS

I don't know which is more discouraging, groundhogs or Standardistos. When our resident groundhog ate eighty percent of my freshly planted, beautiful purple petunias last spring, first I hollered a bit, then I moped. Finally, I went to the hardware store, which, unlike Wal-Mart with its standardized stock, is still a good source of local lore and practical advice. My hardwareman told me to plant a second batch of petunias and bathe them in an epsom salts solution. Then, when the groundhog eats these petunias, the epsom salts will make him sick, and he won't come back. Right. Then I can plant the third set of purple petunias. I don't think so. I'm looking for a solution that won't sacrifice an entire generation of petunias.

Another customer told me to pour kerosene down the groundhog's hole, and he will meet the end he deserves. A second customer told me to chew three sticks of bubble gum and put it in his hole. Then the beast will eat it, the gum will fatally befoul his digestive system, and my petunias will be bothered no more. A third customer had a noise theory: Annoy the groundhog with enough noise and he will head south. All this advice sounds rather like that old Scottish injunction, "First catch your haggis." I mean, I bought the gum, but I never found the groundhog's hole. One day I chased that fat, furry beast up the road. Confessing that I was driving a four-wheel drive vehicle at the time shows how desperate I felt. I know that if I ever find that groundhog's hole, I will chew gum, pour kerosene, play bagpipes, turn cartwheels, and whatever else it takes to keep my petunias safe from predators.

I suspect there might be a moral to this story, and I also suspect different readers will draw different messages from it. Moral-making is never as easy as it sometimes first appears, and I confess to finding different morals on different days. Certainly, there are some noxious creatures at state boards of education across the land, but the teachers and students are the ones being pursued.

All groundhog afficionados should hold their letters of denunciation: I do acknowledge my tenuous position as groundhog pursuer trying to disrupt natural laws. But state boards of education across the land seem to be seeking the triumph of groundhogs over all common sense and decency. Nationwide, they pillage and plunder the estate of our children, taking away by fiat the programs and practices we know to be both developmentally appropriate and necessary.

I would be the first to admit that purple petunias are frivolous. Particularly when one lives in a forest, maybe they are too much of an artifice to be supported. And this is where the moral parallels fall apart. Forget petunias. What Standardistos are trying to sow from coast to coast is a political agenda camouflaged as academic excellence. This is the agenda of a class war that devours the young of the poor as well as the middle- and upper-class young who don't respond well to lock-step commands, i.e., kids who don't want to go to MIT and become technocrats. In addition to devouring the square-hole young, groundhog generals in this war dismiss teachers as irrelevant. For Standardistos, curriculum is all. Once they get their curriculum installed, everything else will fall into place.

THE PERILS OF POMPOUS CATALOGS

Moralizing aside, gardening is a wonderful metaphor for teaching. For starters, we can follow the advice of Henry Ward Beecher. Nineteenth century clergyman, abolitionist, and women's suffragist (okay, he was also a philanderer, but that's another story), Beecher offered advice to gardeners that teachers would do well to heed before they rush to jump on the Standardisto bandwagon. He advised gardeners that they not "be made wild by pompous catalog." This is hard advice to follow, no less in classrooms than in gardens. Disappointing experience notwithstanding, seed catalogs that arrive in the harshness of February continue to tempt me to order by picture and promise, ignoring the reality of living in Zone Two and therefore unable to offer camellias a good home. The Standardistos present presumptions and pomposities every bit as deceptive as those found in any seed catalog. Of course, we are tempted: Who wouldn't want all third graders reading on grade level or all ninth graders holding debates in a foreign language? Reality checks are in order. We must not allow the clamor of the Standardistos to drown out the voices of the children.

Whether Standardistos are hawking NAFTA, which ended up decimating U.S. jobs, or a uniformitarian curriculum, which will end up causing the dropout rate to skyrocket, the language is the same. Standardistos talk in universe-speak, using such cosmic terms as *all workers, children as future workers, global economy, world-class skills, world-class children*. But when they get the phonemes and the math facts all lined up in neat and tidy rows, what Standardistos really offer is a classroom universe of narrow isolationism. They're betting the bank on the *schwa*. The Shakespearean equivalent of their pedagogical cries is, "A schwa! A schwa! My kingdom for a schwa!"

To those who find this too silly to contemplate, I would just point out that plenty of people around the country are willing to sacrifice children's recess period to the voracious skills god. In April of 1998, the *New York Times* carried an article about the growing trend to eliminate recess because it is perceived by persons advocating academic standards as "a waste of time."

A five-year-old in Atlanta confided to a *Times* reporter, "I'd like to sit on the grass and look for ladybugs." But the Atlanta public schools, like a growing number of districts across the country, have eliminated recess from the school day. Who can read this without weeping? The standards mania has brought us to the point of making children too busy for ladybugs. To counter this insanity, the American Association on the Child's Right to Play has been formed.

Benjamin O. Canada, the superintendent of schools in Atlanta, defends the elimination of recess. "We are intent on improving academic performance. You don't do that by having kids hanging on the monkey bars." This is monkey business. Treating a kindergartner like a robot—or a Wall Street broker-in-training—cannot come to a good end. Standardistos don't offer a rich garden of delight; instead, they want us to cut down the meddlesome Spanish moss of curriculum, replacing it with astroturf, which knows how to keep its place.

WHITEWASHING AND SHRINK-WRAPPING DIVERSITY

In the summer of 1998, the City Plannning Committee in San Antonio staged a war against writer Sandra Cisneros' purple house. They say the house, painted Sherwin-Williams Corsican purple, with windows trimmed in aqua, is not in keeping with the surrounding houses located in an historic district. Depending on the beholder, the house is the embodiment of border culture and a symbol of freedom of expression or a flagrant violation of community standards.

Cisneros's purple house is located in an historic Victorian neighborhood, a neighborhood given to white and brown exteriors. The city's Historic Design and Review Commission ruled that even though the Corsican purple is "exquisite," it is historically incorrect and does not meet the neighborhood's standards. Pro-purplists say the issue is about ethnicity. Anti-purplists such as the vice-chairman of the Historical Design and Review Commission, a banker who lives in a brown house, disagrees, saying, "It's not about ethnicity. It's about eccentricity." He adds that it's also about following rules.

I live in a brown and grey house, but I take the battle over the purple house to heart because I know that being a teacher means honoring and nurturing oddball kids, kids who don't meet the neighborhood's standards. Being a teacher means giving kids time and space to work out some kinks. In the name of "preparing the workforce of the twenty-first century," Standardistos insist on a uniformitarian curriculum delivered on schedule; taking a nineteenth century, instrumentalist position, they treat education as a commodity to be regulated (but not paid for) by the government. They see education as something external to the child, as something that can be shrink-wrapped and delivered like meals to a jumbo jet. Even on a jet you usually get a choice of entrees. When Standardistos are in charge, the tastes of teachers and children are irrelevant. Standardistos say, "Eat your liver and Brussels sprouts or go hungry."

DOING WHAT WE CAN

Robert Parker, author of the Spenser detective novels, says, "I write about what I can write about." That's a good mantra for teachers: We teach what we can and how we can. Our challenge is to realize that just because somebody is carrying a hoop doesn't mean we have to jump.

In *Doing Better and Feeling Worse* (W.W. Norton, 1997), Aaron Wildavsky offers telling data about what a medical system can do. The medical system (doctors, drugs, and hospitals) affects just ten percent of the usual indices for measuring a person's health. The remaining ninety percent are determined by factors over which doctors and drugs have little or no control: Smoking, exercise, worry, income, eating habits, genes, air and water quality, and so on.

I wonder if the control percentages are any higher for schools. Standardistos from Cambridge to Chicago to Cupertino, with their blissful faith in half-truths and deliberate obfuscation, would have us believe that all they have to do is write down the skill sequence for success. Then teachers will teach it and students will learn it. This scope-and-sequence chart mentality is far from a new notion in education, but amnesia is an important prerequisite for becoming a Standardisto.

Houston professor Barbara Foorman insists that if a school system chooses the right curriculum, then skills can be delivered to all students. On schedule. According to *The Little Red Reading Book*, a component of the Illinois Right to Read Initiative, published by the Illinois State Board of Education, who hired Foorman as a consultant, when the right skills are delivered, *all students will read above average*, offering a challenge to Lake Wobegon.

In an era of the conspicuous consumption of everything from designer latte to book manuscripts that are grabbed up by publishers and sold to Hollywood before they are even written, "average" has become synonymous with failure. Sports announcers ask Olympic silver medalists how it feels to lose. *The Wall Street Journal* asserts that to be deemed successful you have to be top banana. In a recent promo piece soliciting subscriptions, *Journal* puff writers offer a scenario of the 25-year college reunion of two men. Both are happily married, both work at the same company, but one is deemed "successful," the other not. The failure is only the manager of a small department; the success is president of the company.

What the Standardistos don't seem to grasp is that whether you're talking about national tests or corporate hierarchies, not everybody can—or wants to—be top banana. Some people will be presidents, others will be custodians. We need both. If our society is to function, we need every manner of worker. The shame is not in being a manual laborer, a waitress, or a health-service aide. The shame is that we refuse to pay these people a living wage.

LET'S TALK

Just before he gave a speech, nature writer and all-round iconoclast Edward Abbey was asked to jot down a job description so the person introducing him would know what to say. Abbey described his job as "saving the earth." It is past time for teachers to borrow Abbey's self-description and stake out the territory for saving the earth's children. Not handling them, not training them, but saving them.

The person introducing Abbey was Ronal Carrell Kerbo, chief of cave protection for the National Park Service and a government employee who dared to buck a system run by politicians and corporate commodity honchos. He is profiled in Todd Wilkinson's *Science Under Seige* (Johnson Books, 1998). Teachers who think they can't fight city hall should read this book. Teachers who think they don't have a duty to try should memorize it.

Commenting on Abbey's self-description, Kerbo explained, "There are many of us who feel that way. It doesn't mean that we are martyrs, but we understand that we have to keep talking." The ability to keep talking is the unique strength of people who characterize themselves as whole language teachers: Nobody can shut them up. Kerbo explains why. He says that talk allows "the people who have the passion in their souls to flourish." Continued conversation is our hope for saving the teachers from Standardisto suppression, but to save the children we need action.

2

Standard Timetables for NonStandard Kids

UPSIZING DIAPERS

I wonder if any of the Standardistos has noticed that disposable diapers are getting bigger. Well-known child development expert T. Berry Brazelton appears in TV ads for larger-sized Pampers, diapers made to fit children weighing over thirty-five pounds—the size of a hefty three-year-old. Parents of earlier generations are aghast at evidence of such pokey potty skills: Three years old and still in diapers? I am fascinated to learn that only 22.6 percent of the fast-track toddlers, whose parents are so anxious that they can parrot their ABCs by age two and use a mouse soon afterwards, are toilet trained by the ripe old age of thirty months.

In TV ads for Pampers, Dr. Brazelton promotes the same child-led approach to potty training that he's been advocating for nearly four decades. "Don't rush your toddler into toilet training," Brazelton advises parents, adding, "or let anyone else tell you it's time." As a teacher, I sit back and admire Brazelton's message of respect—both for children and for their parents. I'd like to see "Don't let anyone else tell you it's time" engraved in bronze and hung in school corridors. PTAs could sell "Don't let anyone else tell you it's time" T-shirts, coffee mugs, bumper stickers. But I dream. Instead of being told to relax and get on with their daily lives, children and teachers across the nation are bombarded with the question, "Why are you dragging your feet?" They are told if they don't hurry up, they'll miss out on all those great jobs of the twenty-first century.

I can't let go of the diaper metaphor. In January 1997, the medical journal *Pediatrics* published data showing that by age eighteen months just 0.4 percent of American children are toilet trained. By twenty-four months, the figure is 3.9 percent. Kindergarten teachers can breathe a sign of relief: 97.7 percent of the children in the land are toilet trained by the time they are forty-eight months old. Brazelton insists, of course, that new parents must not look at these figures with the goal of getting their kids into the elite group of gifted toilet trainees. He says toilet training should not be competitive, that it must "be the child's choice." The data indicate that most parents subscribe to Brazelton's standard. Some parents, of course, disagree. An August 1998, *USA Today* article lists potty bribes offered by anxious parents, bribes ranging from M&Ms to tricycles. I confess I wonder what message is sent to a three-year-old when Mama drops Cheerios into the toilet. I also wonder if a Pizza Hut toilet incentive plan is on the horizon.

Brazelton observes that some children are ready to learn to use the potty at age two; others are ready at age four. And guess what? Those who wait until four soon become just as adept in the bathroom as are those precocious early pottyers. Brazelton says that children who are allowed to learn potty use at their own pace gain a sense of accomplishment that's lost when pushy parents resort to threats and bribes. The American Academy of Pediatrics concurs, recommending that parents not worry about the age at which a child is toilet trained but wait until the child is ready.

One can wonder if this generation of toddlers clinging to their diapers doesn't have some sort of metacognitive awareness of what awaits them in the Standardisto's education system. As the standards infestation threatens to reach every corner of the country, deciding when to give up their generous-sized diapers may be the last choice these children will be allowed to make until they graduate from high school. Certainly as soon as they get to kindergarten they will be put on a performance-driven fast track. The refrain, intoned in the manner of a Greek chorus by corporate CEOs, politicians, media pundits, and state boards of education, is that if children can be trained to perform on schedule—meaning phonemes in kindergarten, times tables in third grade, algebra in seventh, then they'll all get jobs in the Fortune 500.

Why people would believe the promises of the fellows who gave us junk bonds, downsizing, and Joe Camel, I don't know. What I do know is that across the land teachers are bowing to the pressure of corporate-politico-infotainment pronouncements: They are eliminating recess and putting away the building blocks, the tempera paints, and the picture books that don't introduce phonemes in the sequence chosen by the publishing conglomerate so venerated in Texas and California. They are bringing out the skill drill worksheets that will get every kid in America learning the schwa on schedule.

This is a two-fold disaster. To barter the present lives of young children for some promise of future job security is a delusion and a fraud. Even worse is to usurp the joy of childhood in the name of a national obsession to score first on a mathematics test that not one person in ten thousand knows anything about. Our jobs as teachers is to see to the present lives of children, and that's a job plenty big enough. To treat kindergartners, third graders, seventh graders as if they were objects on a conveyer belt to the future goes against the American grain. One could hope that child advocates might find some corporate maverick or other monied patron to finance TV ads proclaiming curriculum choices to be at least as important as potty choices. Wal-Mart heirs dedicate millions to undermining the public school system; we need to find some deep-pocketed idealist who will support it. Lacking that, we teachers must continue to offer children the choices they need to thrive, and we must continue to tell our stories.

RITALIN ROUTINES

As Erma Bombeck observed, "Suburbs are small, controlled communities where for the most part everyone has the same living standards, the same number of garbage cans, the same house plans, and the same level in the septic tanks." She should have added, "And their kids all learn the times tables in third grade." In the nineties, if a white, middle- to upper-middle-class suburbanite kid doesn't memorize his multiplication tables on schedule, his parents demand Ritalin, fearing that the child who doesn't keep step with the academic schedule might not get that job in the Fortune 500. Although I promise not to carry the metaphor to its logical conclusion, I have spent a lot of time with various standards documents from around the country and I can show that the standards edicts gushing forth from state boards of education have a lot in common with septic tanks.

In *Running on Ritalin* (Bantam, 1998), Lawrence Diller, professor at

University of California at San Francisco and a behavioral pediatrician, raises some provocative questions about our performance-driven culture, a culture that fuels the spiraling demand for Ritalin. Diller notes that since 1990 the number of children and adults diagnosed with attention deficit disorder (ADD), the condition for which Ritalin is most commonly prescribed, has risen from nine hundred thousand to almost five million. During the same time period there has been a seven hundred percent increase in the amount of Ritalin, a controlled substance, produced in the U.S.

Ritalin, of course, is not new. In *The Myth of the Hyperactive Child* (Dell, 1975), Peter Schrag and Diane Divoky documented the uses of Ritalin to keep children in line. Middle-class white kids were labeled Learning Disabled, poor black kids pre-delinquent. Both groups got Ritalin. Proponents of the wholesale drugging of children insisted that deviations from the norm are caused by some small brain dysfunction that can be smoothed out by drugs. Experts determine that a child can't control himself, can't alter his behavior, and he is given Ritalin to do the job for him. In 1971, a report from the U.S. Department of Health, Education, and Welfare estimated that three percent of the school-age population suffered from moderate or severe hyperkinesis. But as in so many things, California quickly jumped out in front. A 1974 staff report to the chairman of the Education Committee of the California State Senate put the figure of hyperactive kids in the Golden State at fifteen percent. As Schrag and Divoky observe, there's nothing new about teachers and parents complaining that children are difficult to control and to teach. What is new is saying these children have a clearly definied medical syndrome, a syndrome that should be treated with amphetamines.

Although there's nothing new about schools wanting kids who can't sit still to be given a pill to help them conform to classroom norms, the Ritalin explosion of the nineties seems to have another component. It is no coincidence that this drug deluge parallels the standards explosion of the same period. Ritalin is the drug of choice for people worried their children might be "underachievers," a term I must admit I have never understood. What I do understand is that the trickle-down theory of academic competitiveness and preparing kids for their SATs means that kindergartners no longer have time to play. Maine, heretofore regarded as a state with a sane and sensible education system, now has standards with 178 indicators for kindergarten success. On March 22, 1842, Henry David Thoreau wrote in his journal, "Nothing can be more useful to a man than a determination not to be hurried." I would borrow his sentiment and say that nothing can be more useful to a

child than to be in the classroom of a teacher who has a determination neither a hurried nor a hurrier to be.

Diller observes that we are making far greater demands of children
than we used to, pointing out that "Subjects such as multiplication and division are introduced a year earlier than in the curriculum of twenty-five years
ago." He writes that a child with a "spirited temperament" might be able to
function well enough in a less stressful environment. But parents are reluctant to opt out of the fast-track system for their children. And, of course,
schools can't reduce their standards. So the kids get pills.

Parents are somewhat ambivalent about the increased workload their
children carry. They can see what the added stress is doing to their children,
and parents complain almost as much as kids about finding time to get all
the homework done. Teachers report that they hear few of these com-
plaints. After all, with media complicity, the politico-industrial-infotain-
ment complex bombards us with that message of the direct links between
academic success and future economic success, so it becomes a parent's
duty to keep those kids running on the treadmill. The result is that children
feel more and more hurried, imitating the frazzled lives of their parents
who, as study after study shows, are working harder to keep their standard
of living from sliding further.

The issue is not that bad people put their kids on Ritalin and good
people don't. I remember with sinking heart my third graders, the low readers the school had clumped together as losers, accosting their classmate
who, at 11:15 in the morning, was flying around the room with his arms
spread wide, set off by my reading a story about a hawk. "Bobby, take your
pills!" When Bobby's mother was short of cash and couldn't buy his "fix,"
we all suffered. I felt guilty every day I thanked God—or the school's hack
psychologist—for Ritalin, but nonetheless I did know that the other children and I needed for Bobby to have it. My need was probably at least as
great as his.

The Standardistos who proclaim that teachers and their students are
both lazy and stupid refuse to acknowledge the tremendous pressures put on
both teachers and students. We expect an incredible amount of "stuff" from
our students. In our own era of downsizing and outsizing, we're frightened
about our children's future, so we insist that things will work out if the kids
just study metamorphic rocks in third grade and algebra in seventh. The awful truth is that teaching research paper skills has moved down to second
grade. For years, I have proclaimed, "If Harvard wants them to write research
papers, let Harvard teach them." But I was talking about seventh graders.

The delicious craziness of seven-year-olds learning to cite references leaves me (almost) speechless.

I wonder why nobody ever mentions poetry or music as a necessity for the successful citizen. No doubt Japan's economic woes in the late 1990s will reduce our frantic efforts to make our schools more like theirs, but at the height of the "copy Japan" imperative, nobody was mentioning that everybody in Japan learns to write haiku. All sorts of people who should know better claim that the secret of Japan's success is the way they teach mathematics. And wear uniforms.

Similarly, you don't hear Standardistos talking about the system of social promotion in Japan. There, forty children enter school together and they stay together, moving along as a group, until the end of sixth grade. By definition, that group learns on schedule. The teacher does not permit anyone to move ahead nor acknowledge that anybody might have fallen behind. When I asked members of the Tokyo Board of Education about this, I was assured that group identity keeps kids together and prevents anyone from falling behind. When Japanese parents were asked what they expect the schools to teach their children, 98.3 percent cited the discipline of group life.

After sixth grade, things change, and they change dramatically. Suddenly the Japanese educational system takes this carefully nurtured, homogeneous group and rates individual members. All sixth graders take a highly competitive exam to get into choice high schools that will provide the ticket to prestigious colleges and desirable employment. Parents go somewhat berserk over this test, putting their children into intensive after-school cram classes. One of my favorite souvenirs from Japan is a newspaper ad for a study carrel for the home, complete with bell for Junior to summon Mom so that she can bring him whatever he needs, when he needs it. It is an interesting twist on the American "feed on demand" practice. But as bad as the sixth grade exam may be, children in Japan are given six years of guaranteed success. Social promotion is at the heart of their schooling. Nobody fails. There are no pictures on nightly TV of Japanese fourth graders attending summer school with the threat that if they don't pass a standardized test, they won't go on to fifth grade.

CURSED RITUALS

My students cried when I introduced Cursive. So did I. Cursive is always referred to that way in third grade—with a capital C. Cursive. What a word. What a burden. Since I didn't have a clue how to teach Cursive, I followed the manual. You could say I followed it to the letter of the law. The students moaned and groaned. Leslie wept tears worthy of an operatic diva; Larry vomited. After three weeks, I couldn't take it any more. I quit. I stuck the manual back in the closet and told the kids to keep on printing. And they did.

In mid-March an interesting change began to occur. Every so often when a student asked me to spell a word on the board, she'd add, "Write it in cursive." Then one day Leslie demanded, "How come we aren't learning cursive?"

As any teacher not being pursued by Standardistos would, I scrapped my planned schedule and put my pedagogical antennae on immediate high alert. Call it what you will, the teachable moment, the bird in the window, at the core of being a teacher is the ability to listen when children speak, to understand and act on their sometimes obvious but often very subtle messages. I told Leslie, "As a matter of fact, we're starting cursive today. Right this minute." I promptly wrote their spelling words on the board in cursive and invited them to try to copy what I'd done.

There may well be research indicating that such a strategy is the worst tactic possible. But about such matters I have the same attitude as most veteran teachers. In public relations it's called Gibson's Law: For every Ph.D. there's an equal and opposite Ph.D. I'm in the classroom at this very minute. Of course I must make my decisions as savvy and as humane as possible, but in the end, we teachers cannot live by rules: Dogma cannot carry us through the thousands of individual teaching decisions of the day. One of my mantras is that a teacher can only teach who she is. To make the decisions about classroom events ever-swarming around us, we have to rely on our own educated intuition. I didn't dig out the manual, and I'll admit the children learned the letters in a rather haphazard fashion. One pedagogical camp would call my method "individualistic"; another would call it "screwball." And they both would be right.

All through the day, whenever someone asked for a specific letter, I'd go to the board and write it. Sometimes I'd say, "OK, drop what you're doing and try a "g." Some kids would follow the letter of the law and write one "g." The ever-enthusiastic Leslie would usually fill a page with whatever letter was called for. All children quickly learned to write their names and then I pronounced them experts on those letters, available to give lessons when one of their peers ran into trouble. Leslie would walk around the room offering her skills, rather like the itinerant medieval scholars. "Do you want to learn capital L? I can show you how to make beautiful capital L's." Then some children began to ask for cursive renditions of the poems I'd been printing on the board since the first day of school, poems they were required to copy in their poetry notebooks. I felt like a translator at the United Nations, putting everything on the board in two versions.

A few weeks into this cursive enterprise, I compared the cursive production of my class, designated the lowest readers in third grade, with two other classes, children who had been painstakingly practicing official Cursive all year. There didn't seem to be all that much difference. There were a few stars in each group and also a few children who had not made a good transition. But most of my low group had made the transition, and they had made it painlessly. I tell this story as a small "proof" that we teachers can resist the Standardisto imperative that would turn us into train conductors, programmed to keep our students operating on an ideal schedule devised by a complicity of politicians and bureaucrats. As teachers, we must resist much. We must also tell these stories. We must tell them often, and we must tell them loudly.

In reflecting on this story years after the event, I realize my resistance to putting too much importance on Cursive came early in life. I learned Cursive in first grade—from a real termagant, the stereotypical old battle-axe schoolmarm. Although I was a stellar student, only getting my hand smacked with the ruler once—when I passed scissors the wrong way—I was very aware of how much this teacher scared some kids. My strongest memory of first grade is of two big boys who couldn't read the Dick and Jane words when the teacher pointed her long wooden pointer at them. About once a week one or the other of those boys wet his pants when she waved that pointer in his direction. The teacher would leave the puddle of failure and embarrassment on the floor all day. I remember trying to avoid looking at the floor.

My second strongest memory is being asked to stay in during recess and teach one of those boys how to make a capital I in Cursive. He worked hard, filling all the blackboards in the room with capital I's in which the bottom loop swung out to the right instead of to the left. When our teacher returned, she had a fit. "Susan! What's wrong with you? You know how to make capital I's. Why did you let him make them all backwards?"

I didn't reply, but I remember being indignant. She knew and I knew that those were capital I's. They contained all the elements of the giant capital I on the cardboard strip of letters running along the top of the board. So what difference did it make which way the bottom loop went? I guess I've never wanted to let myself get bogged down by petty details.

Our town had no kindergarten, and I'd barely scraped by the age requirement for first grade. I had some serious and chronic health problems, and my mother was apprehensive about how I'd do. Years later, when I was myself a teacher, my mother asked me if I remembered being turned into a right-hander in first grade. She told me that before I started school I was left-handed. About three months into first grade, she noticed I was using my right hand. In those days, parents were convinced that "the school knows best" and that they shouldn't interfere, so my mother never said a word. Not to my teacher, not to me. I have no recollection of being forced to change from left- to right-handedness. I would guess that my five-year-old self figured that's how school was 'spozed to be. After all, every day I saw worse things happening to other kids, the kids who were so scared they peed in their pants. I probably figured the teacher devised a different torture for each kid. Or maybe I thought it was illegal to do Cursive with your left hand. Looking back all these decades later, I wonder if those boards filled with wrong-sided capital I's weren't the small revenge of a five-year-old left-hander.

Standardistos like to claim that kids these days aren't learning as much as kids used to. As I write these words, I'm listening to the economist Milton Friedman make the case on National Public Radio for a free market school system. Easy quotes from *A Nation at Risk* (National Commission on Excellence in Education, 1983) roll off his tongue as he insists that for the first time in our nation's history this generation is worse educated than the preceding generation. In not bothering to acknowledge that we didn't even try to educate everybody in preceding generations, Friedman echoes every Standardisto who seems to think that standards plummeted the day he received his high school diploma.

Once I got out of first grade, what I remember about school is having a good time. We put on plays and painted and sang. In fifth grade, we all learned to knit; in sixth grade, our teacher taught us to play the harmonica, and because we loved him and because he was an ex-Marine, we secretly learned to play "The Marine's Hymn" for his birthday. When spirits got high inside the classroom, we went outside and pounded on tetherballs. Today, kids don't even get recess. Nobody is going to convince me that in the good old days my classmates and I worked harder in school than today's kids do.

THE MOMENT OF RIPENESS

I wonder which Standardisto will step forward to pass judgment on Carol—or on me. Despite all my efforts, Carol didn't read a book all year, not one.

Oh, I could pull her along with her classmates through the Iroquois worksheets I'd prepared to help them make some sense of their unbelievably fatuous social studies textbook. I knew just how fatuous that text was because, during a weekend of sanctimonious, self-prescribed martyrdom, I took home all my students' "content area" textbooks and I read them. It was the next-to-worst weekend of my life, superseded only by the great ice storm of 1998, when my household went a week without electricity, heat, water, and flushing toilets.

Carol and I did not manage to find a book that made words sing for her; we never even found words to make her smile. Carol kept to herself. She was silent and uncommunicative both with me and with the other students. I remember just one exchange she had with another student all year. Ofelia was complaining about her mother being too strict. "She thinks she can still hit me, but I'm taller than her now." Carol, the loner who never participated in classroom conversations, Carol, the pasty pale girl with stringy dirty-blonde hair, always wearing a heavy dark sweatshirt, making no concessions to fashion among a group of seventh graders who were obsessed by clothes and style, Carol stirred in her chair and announced vehemently, "My mother better not come near me or the cops will lock her up again." For seven months, I had never seen Ofelia, obsessed with her rings and her nail decals and her corn rows and the lace inserts in her jeans, acknowledge Carol's existence, but now she was curious, "Who you live with, your grandmother?"

"No way!" declared Carol. "She's worse than my mother. I live with a foster mother. She better not touch me neither."

Eyes downcast, Carol slumped back down in her chair, and that ended the conversation. I found out later that this child had been so abused as an infant that she'd been taken out of her home at age two. According to faculty-room lore, part of the abuse involved setting her in a frying pan on the stove. I didn't stick around to hear any more.

In the way schools are judged, even in the way I judge myself, Carol was one of my failures. She came to me not caring about books and she left the same way. Nonetheless, at the end of the year Carol offered me one brief crystal moment, a moment that still sparkles more than two decades later. Maybe I should call it one oatmeal moment. The seventh and eighth graders, who occupied the top floor of a three-story brick fortress of a building, heard that classes on the floors beneath us were having end-of-the-year parties; they insisted that we had to have one too. My colleagues said that the nasty rotten kids didn't deserve a party, and so I was on my own.

I don't know how many cookies I baked in the three nights before the last day of school, but it was definitely an industrial-strength effort. Every kid and his out-of-town cousin showed up to wish me a good summer—and to eat a cookie. Jimmy, whom I'd regarded as terminally lethargic, must have eaten two dozen. Every time the bell rang to signal a change in classes, Jimmy dashed by, calling out, "Hey, Miz O," and grabbing another cookie or two.

By the time my afternoon classes arrived, all the chocolate chip cookies were gone, leaving only oatmeal with raisins. Danny, Delmore, and even the prissy and proper Roderick were indignant. "Where's the chocolate chip? It ain't fair! How come everybody else got chocolate chip and all we got is rank oatmeal?" The girls didn't say anythng but sniffed their refusal of the oatmeal cookies.

I held back tears of frustration and anger. Who needed this grief? Try to do something nice, and all these nasty rotten kids can do is complain. I knew I was setting myself as victim, which is always a losing role for a teacher, but why did these kids have to spoil things?

Then Carol, still wearing her dark heavy sweatshirt in our sweltering, end-of-June classroom, walked over and touched my arm. "Those are good oatmeal cookies." She actually smiled, this child who hadn't smiled all year. Carol smiled and she said, "Could I have another one?" The child whose reading scores remained abysmal gave me the gift of empathy and compassion. And now, reflecting on this incident so many years later, I think maybe I did help her learn something after all. I couldn't enter it on her permanent record card. Carol's gesture won't appear on any chart of world-class skills or on any test certifying teacher competencies. But can anyone doubt that Carol took an essential step forward? My guess is that she had to learn to smile before she could learn to read. Certainly she had to be able to put herself in someone else's shoes—even the shoes of a teacher—before she could have any hope for a satisfying and productive life.

Politicians, corporate leaders, media pundits, and education entrepreneurs don't talk about social responsibility. Perhaps they realize if they dared to start orating about teachers' social responsibility, the public would laugh them out of the halls. Who knows? Maybe even the great mass of teachers, who currently shut their doors, hoping the Standardistos' rampage across the land will wear itself out before it does too much harm, would get angry enough to protest. Recently I heard a teacher who is a leader in reform mathematics say three times in a presentation about the wonderful results stemming from the reform curriculum she uses that the only hope for the continuing life of this program lies with who gets elected governor.

In any case, politicians, corporate leaders, media pundits, and education entrepreneurs don't talk about compassion, about caring, about creativity, curiosity, initiative, self-reliance, or myriad other qualities that we must nurture in our students. I think it's time to ask the Standardistos: Where's the test for compassion? For honesty? For curiosity? For moral commitment? Until they can answer, let's tell them to shut up.

THE WEIRDEST KIDS IN FOURTH GRADE

Newbery Medalist Katherine Paterson speaks passionately for the diversity of children's needs. In *The Spying Heart* (Dutton, 1989), she tells a story that would wring tears from a turnip, tears of joy and wonder in the face of an oddball child's triumph. Paterson recalls her fourth-grade year, an awful year, "a time of almost unmitigated terror and humiliation," a year she acknowledges having drawn upon throughout her writing career. She recalls a classmate, a fourth grader who was "the other weird kid in the fourth grade," Eugene Hammett, who, she recalls, unlike her, a child who couldn't help her funny name and the fact that she was born in China, was "weird by choice."

"Eugene's declared ambition was to become a ballet dancer. In North Carolina in 1941, little boys—even well-built or skinny little boys—did not want to be ballet dancers when they grew up." Gene was not skinny. Katherine Womeldorf and Eugene Hammett were friends through fourth, fifth, sixth, and seventh grades. By seventh grade, says Katherine, "I had fulfilled my modest ambition. I was no longer regarded as particularly weird. Eugene, having more integrity, continued to march, or should I say dance, to a different drummer."

Katherine moved, and never saw Eugene again. Jump ahead to her adult life. Living in Norfork, Virginia, her seventeen-year-old son, a serious actor, needs to take dancing lessons. But even in 1983, boys in Norfolk, Virginia don't aspire to be ballet dancers, and Katherine's son asks her to find out "about lessons he can take without the rest of the soccer team knowing about it." Katherine asks around and discovers that "Gene Hammett at Tidewater Ballet is really the best teacher around." He is described as a former New York City dancer, "a bit weird," a huge figure in great flowing caftans, and a wonderful teacher. Katherine sees pictures of him "leaping like Baryshnikov," looking not at all like the chubby, bespectacled boy she knew in fourth grade.

Katherine gets in touch with Gene, asking if he remembers her. He says he even remembers the joke she told in fourth grade. Politicians, corporate leaders, media pundits, and education entrepreneurs would ask how Eugene's math scores compared with those of the Japanese before they judged him successful.

In "Self-Reliance," Ralph Waldo Emerson tells us that character teaches above our wills, that "virtue or vice emit breath at every moment." Now this is scary stuff. If we take Emerson to heart and believe that, with every breath, teachers send out rays of virtue or vice, why aren't we more worried about the character of the people running our schools than about finding a test that will show us if students in Alaska are ahead of those in Vermont in apostrophe acquisition?

Katherine Paterson quotes Flannery O'Connor, who said, "Fiction is about everything human and we are made out of dust, and if you scorn getting yourself dusty, then you shouldn't write fiction. It isn't grand enough for you." What a great description of teaching. Teaching is about everything human, and those who insist on looking only at intellectual abstractions, scorning getting themselves dusty with the rough-and-tumble of a child's reality, should not try it. Nor should they write grand rules for teachers to follow. But when they do write their grand rules, we must follow Henry David Thoreau's advice and "resist much."

3

Standard Fare: The Rich Get Richer, the Poor Get Ignored

HOOKED ON HYPE

Standardistos proclaim that standards are in and of them-selves a guarantee of educational equity. State commis-sioners of education promise that standards won't be watered down for anybody. Therefore, by fiat, everybody will achieve equal excellence. And get that Fortune 500 job. Creating new skills empires in the name of excellence for all, raising the bar for high school graduation, is at best an empty promise; at worst, it is criminal malfeasance. Handing out standards in the name of preparing everyone to meet the high skills that will be demanded for employment in the twenty-first century is as cynical as hand-ing out menus to homeless people in the name of eradicating hunger. Does it matter how carefully the menu calibrates its offer-ings to the federal Food Pyramid, advising people to be sure to choose 6–11 daily servings from the bread/cereal/rice/pasta group, 3–5 servings from the vegetable group, 2–4 servings from the fruit group, and so on?

Let them eat cake. Let them take calculus.

The attitude of saying, "Not my students!" puts people like

31

me in a box labelled *Catch-22*. Today it is not fashionable to say that some students can learn to use trigonometric functions and some can't. I really don't want to argue about who will and who won't take calculus or read *Hamlet*. I want us to sit down and discuss at what age we start training kids to think that if they don't go to college, they will be failures. I want us to ask at what cost comes telling kids that if they don't score 1500 on the SAT, their lives are over. When I interviewed parents in Ames, Iowa about their attitudes toward math reform in the middle grades, several themes emerged. A vocal group of parents opposed the heterogeneous groupings of reform, and as a way of avoiding it, pushed their children into seventh-grade algebra.

Traditionally, students in Ames who take algebra before ninth grade are graded pass/fail. Parents worry about a recent decision to administer letter grades in eighth-grade algebra. Ironically, Standardisto parents worry that instituting the standards of grades might damage academic sure bets. Parents want their children to take algebra early and they don't worry about whether this subject will speak to eleven- and twelve-year-olds on the profound and intuitive level that might enhance their lives; they worry over whether a less-than-perfect score in the subject, the reality of entering high school with the deficit implied by a grade of "B," will ruin the possibility of their child's demonstrating to college admissions a record of perfection in high school.

The worry of such parents is merely an aside in the standards wars; national standards and measures aren't made for the elite schools in the nation. The elite have always used different yardsticks from the rest of us. Students in elite public high schools take Chinese in sixth grade, algebra in seventh. In high school, their schedules are crammed with advanced placement, college credit courses. As Jay Mathews notes in *Class Struggle* (Times Books, 1998), there is instruction of "unprecedented rigor and complexity" in America's elite public high schools. The desire to please their parents and to gain admission into the nation's prestigious colleges both inspires and impels these students to work hard and to do well.

IF YOU WANT TO DO WELL IN SCHOOL, MAKE SURE YOUR PARENTS DID WELL

Plenty of research studies show that there is no better predictor of success in school than the level of schooling attained by one's parents. And the best predictor of wealth is several previous generations of wealth in the family. So inheritance, not curriculum, not teacher quality, is the greatest predictor of school success. But parents of kids already on the fast track to success support national standards that are irrelevant to their children; such standards let those who were born with the gold standards in their mouth off the hook of moral responsibility to be their brother's keeper. Standardistos can insist on their belief in democracy: "We offered everybody the same standards. It isn't our fault if you didn't pass calculus."

National and state and district standards harm teachers as well as children. As John Goodlad has observed, "the schools of the wealthy ghetto, whether public or private, do not have to try very hard to be regarded as excellent on the criteria of test scores and admission of graduates to elite college and universities." My experience is that the best, most hard-working teachers in a district often work in the poverty schools, the schools with the lowest test scores. Admittedly, that's often where the worst teachers work, too. But there is no small irony in the fact that when parents settle for high standardized test scores as proof of excellence, they might well be settling for mediocre teaching.

I gained some local fame when one of the third graders in my class of rotten readers scored 100 percent on the Stanford reading test. It's a long, complicated story, but Billy was in low reading because from kindergarten on, he ate his pencils rather than put any marks on papers. He was a voracious reader, but since he refused to fill out any of the phonics worksheets, he was put into low reading. Because he loved getting daily notes from me, Billy did write notes. His penmanship and spelling were the worst I have ever seen. I knew he was not going to survive in school if he didn't stop eating the pencils and start doing some routine school work, so I asked the help of a resource teacher who ran her classroom along strict, behaviorist principles. We traded students: She took Billy and I took Charles, a developmentally delayed eleven-year-old with severe emotional problems. I explain all this to point out that Billy, who scored 100 percent on the reading comprehension portion of the test, had no reading "instruction" all year. He stopped by my room to borrow books, and occasionally I'd grab him and ask him about what he was reading. That was it.

The troubling issue is that at the same time people will acknowledge that most ghetto schools are not good places to be, few realize that schools perceived to be excellent by all of IBM chief Louis Gerstner's "output" standards are often quite vicious places for children to be. In any case, teachers are both rewarded and punished for something over which they have no control—the kids who walk in the door.

Parents like the idea of schools infusing hyperskills into the classrooms, skills that promise to make their kids world class while the parents sit at home watching mudwrestling on TV or spend their evenings working at their high-power jobs, invisible to their children. According to a national survey, in 1997, parents talked to their children 38.5 minutes a week. Those same children watch television 1,680 minutes each week. I have a modest proposal: Since the schools can't do it all, we should use Goals 2000 funds to build Skill Theme Parks: Superhighways to Standards. Thirty-eight lanes to World-Class Skills. There'd be Bumper Car Blends, Ye Olde Schwa Museum and Gift Shoppe, and, well, you get the idea. This could be accompanied by public service announcements on TV: It's 10 o'clock. Do you know where your kids' math facts are?

STANDARDISTOS OFFER WHOLESALE

As I reported in the pages of *Phi Delta Kappan* more than a decade ago (September, 1988), then-Secretary of Education William Bennett cut to the heart of the Standardisto doctrine when he responded to a school board member's question after a speech he delivered in Allentown, Pennsylvania, "How is all this going to work?," with "I deal with wholesale; you're going to have to work out the retail for yourself." There you have it: Standardistos don't give a damn about how their plans and panaceas might work in classrooms.

Truth in disclosure: I couldn't come close to passing the ambitious "draft" standards of one of our large states, a state with a diverse multicultural population, a state with large rural areas as well as troubled urban ones. Here's a brief sampling: In science, all ninth graders will be expected to understand the structure of atomic nuclei; in math, students will solve linear and quadratic equations. In social studies, students must explain "how processes of spatial change have affected history." Ninth graders are expected to lead discussion groups in a foreign language. And if anyone needs proof that the standards game is ever escalating: Ninth graders are also expected to write the dreaded research paper—in a foreign language.

Does anybody believe that the fellows who wrote this stuff had met many ninth graders? These same "draft" standards declare that children in the primary grades will "make inferences based on information in print media"—in a foreign language. Gentle reader, how many primary graders do you know who can make inferences in their mother tongue? How many administrators?

There are lots more pompous pronouncements about what students *will* achieve in the fine arts and in history, and then comes the final insanity: In physical education, ninth graders will "achieve improved health-related fitness" through a physical fitness program they design. Does this mean fat-sos won't graduate?

I love the fact that the district where I used to teach in upstate New York declares that second graders will master nouns, third graders verbs, and fifth graders adverbs. Third graders master poetry, fifth graders science fiction. Like many standards documents, this one contains a lot of "will" statements.

- Students will have a strong grammar foundation and will be able to demonstrate good usage and mechanics in their writing.

- Students will follow the rules for listening.

Pardon me? How many teachers do you know who follow the rules for listening? Probably teachers are such poor listeners because nobody listens to them. For that matter, just what are the rules for listening?

This is not to say that local officials deal with "retail" any better than state Standardistos. Local officials draw arrows to show how standards will work:

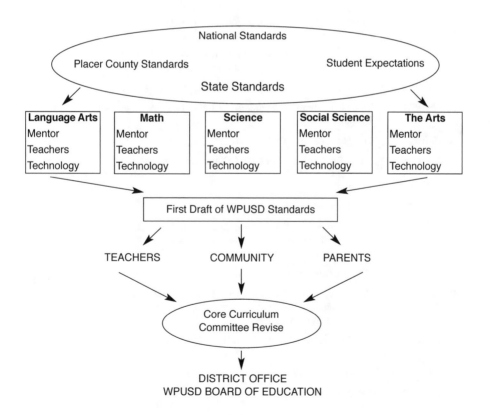

Statewide Faculty Meeting Resource Packet
September 3, 1996

**STATEWIDE
FACULTY MEETING**

TEACHER-TO-TEACHER:
MAKING HIGHER STANDARDS COME TO LIFE

Program Summary

10:00–10:03*	Program Opening Introduction of Panel, Live Audience, Commissioner Mills Opening Discussion, Moderator/Commissioner: "Higher Expectations, No Exceptions"
10:03–10:10	Video Presentation, Teacher & Classroom Perspectives: "What is the Most Significant Challenge of Higher Standards for All"
10:10–10:17	Live Discussion: "The Challenge of Higher Standards"
10:17–10:19	Viceo Presentation: "Standards: What's Next? (A Schedule of Coming Events)"
10:19–10:21	Live Discussion: "What's Next?"
10:21–10:28	Video Presentation, Teacher & Classroom Perspectives: "What Can I Do,Starting Today, To Make Higher Standards Come to Life?"
10:28–10:35	Live Discussion: "What Can I Do?"
10:35–10:37	Video Presentation, Teacher & Classroom Perspectives: "How Will Standards Affect Testing, Assessment?"
10:37–10:43	Live Discussion "Standards and Assessment?"

10:43–10:45	Video Presentation, Teacher & Classroom Perspectives:
	  Resources: "What Do We Have, What Do We Need,
	  To Make Standards Work?"

10:45–10:52	Live Discussion: "What Do We Have, What Do We Need?"
10:52–10:59	Live Discussion: Conclusions, Wrap-up
10:59–11:00	Closing Credits

At the state level, they hold video conferences, allotting seven minutes for presentation of teacher and classroom perspectives on each topic.

STANDARDS WINDCHILL FACTOR

One can understand why the WPUSD superintendent hopes to draw a few arrows and be done with the latest state standards: After all, the average shelf life of a set of standards is three years, two months, seventeen days, and forty-three minutes. A school shelf life differs from a home shelf life in that items on school shelves rarely cause botulism. The shelf life dangers connected with schools are slow and debilitating. They take a kid's spirit over time rather than offering dramatic extinction within 48 hours.

But I need to be realistic here. Most teachers don't worry nearly so much about standards as I do. For teachers in the classroom right this minute, standards come pretty low down on the list of things that annoy, irritate, and worry. Just ask yourself where you'd put standards on this list of teacher concerns.

Squirrely students

Passive students

Students who don't do their homework

Pushy parents

Parents who don't push enough

Inability to get a class set of dictionaries

Disappearance of the adapter plug

Quality of food in the cafeteria

School-wide absence of toilet paper

October absence of orange construction paper

A classroom clock that hasn't worked in eight years

Making sure your students score as well on math tests as students in Singapore

Likewise, standards come pretty low down on the list of things that annoy, irritate, and worry parents. Just ask yourself, where do standards fit on this list of things that concern you about your children?

Organizing the car pool to get kids to after-school practice

Trying to find a cub-scout den mother

Teachers who assign too much homework

Teachers who don't assign enough homework

Not understanding your child's homework

A child who doesn't do his homework

Bossy teachers

Teachers with unlisted phone numbers

Condition of the child's bedroom

Fighting with siblings

A child's not writing a thank-you note for the birthday present your mother-in-law sent eight months ago

Making sure your child scores as well on math tests as children in Singapore

If there are more than six teachers in the country who don't worry more about the health of the classroom goldfish than about the hyped-up notion of "world-class standards" for their students, I'll eat both the goldfish and the standards. In any case, I challenge anybody to walk into a faculty room and read their state standards aloud.

A MILLION-DOLLAR BABY

If my old district takes the low road, copying their so-called standards from the table of contents of a third-rate languge arts textbook, the *Standards for the English Language Arts*, a million-dollar joint project of the National Council of Teachers of English and the International Reading Association (1996) got smeared in the press for trying to take the high road. Truth in disclosures: From the get-go, I have been against NCTE's role in the politically charged project of creating a standards document. My own participation in two summer *Standards* retreats sponsored by NCTE made me feel worse, not better, about the endeavor.

I have been against the *Standards* for political as well as personal reasons. I think it is dishonest and demeaning to imply that we English teachers haven't had standards before now. It is dishonest and demeaning to imply that twelve language arts tenets will lift students out of poverty, give them equal educational opportunity, or even improve the education being offered to them. It is morally bankrupt to cooperate with politicians and corporate CEOs in preaching "world-class standards" while burying the real problems of political malfeasance, corporate greed, and the shocking number of children living in poverty under a cloud of semantic obfuscation. Such tactics lead to the deforming rather than the reforming of educational opportunity.

The introduction to *Standards for the English Language Arts* makes passing reference, in an unfortunately whiny tone, to the fact that not all schools are equal in condition of the buildings and availability of supplies. Nonetheless, by its purpose and nature, this treatise, which cost one million dollars to produce and which claims that its very existence is necessary to "bridge the documented disparities that exist in educational opportunities," ignores the brutal truth about so many of our schools. This truth is documented with devastating clarity by Jonathan Kozol in *Savage Inequalities* (Crown, 1991). Everybody would be much better informed about the real education standards in the United States by reading Kozol than by reading the plethora of institutional standards documents which, like NCTE's, have an ax to grind and territory to protect. I doubt that anyone reading these institutional document walks away thinking the primary concern is for children.

From the get-go I viewed the NCTE standards with great misgivings because I feared what such a endeavor would do to the organization to which I feel both longtime gratitude and fierce loyalty. NCTE has played an important role in my professional life. The people I see at NCTE conventions are the people who have informed my professional work as a teacher. So I was dismayed from the early beginnings of this standards project when it was clear that bad things were going to happen to good intentions. One obvious pitfall is our professional jargon. Terms such as *emergent literacy, performance-oriented instruction, constructing meaning, literacy event, literary traditions that contextualize literary texts, peer writing, visual systems out of which texts are created,* and *authentic learning experiences* seem to roll easily off the tongues of some people. Although this is a language I do not speak, I have heard people I respect insist that such specialized language is both important and necessary. They don't seem to care that everybody outside our small community is left clueless when faced with such syllabub.

I confess to being a semantic yokel when it comes to professional jargon. Even when some of my good friends utter a word like "rubric," I immediately transpose myself to another sphere, a comfort zone serviced by solid

New England Puritan sorts of words. I just never have been able to snuggle up to professionalese. So I speak from very personal experience when I observe that it is both ironic and boneheaded for people devoted to the teaching and learning of English to issue a document calling for the general public to participate in a "shared vision" of language arts and then employ an opaque writing style that will leave both the majority of teachers and all of the public baffled.

A press kit accompanying the NCTE/IRA Standards contains enthusiastic blurbs for the document, but they come from education insiders who probably worked on the standards, people the public have reason to suspect of having a vested interest: An administrator at the Hawaii Department of Education, a professor at the University of Iowa, a vice-president of Educational Testing Service. The fact that there is no indication that the document was reviewed or supported by people in business, industry, the arts, media, or politics is an unfortunate ethical as well as tactical blunder. NCTE and IRA insist the document is for insiders, for English teachers. The subtitle on the cover states *For the Profession, By the Profession: A Guide for Discussion*. But who's talking to whom? And for what purpose?

Any standards document worth its salt must be a public document. Ironically, the National Council of Teachers of Mathematics produced a standards document that is eminently more readable than the English teachers' document. And to make sure that the public would applaud their document, NCTM spent $500,000 on upfront public relations. NCTM hired Madison Avenue experts, and the culminating event prior to the public unveiling was for organization leaders to spend half a day in the editorial offices of *The New York Times*, *The Wall Street Journal*, *The Los Angeles Times*, and so on. One might suspect that the media loved NCTM's standards as much for the fact that they are intimidated by mathematics as for the fact that a savvy PR campaign was staged, but nobody can deny that NCTM's standards make for convincing, comprehensible reading.

In contrast, the *Standards for the English Language Arts* was a political hot potato right from the start. After all, the federal government funded its creation and then, not liking the way the document was shaping up, withdrew the money. This gives an indication of the tenor of Goals 2000: Do it our way or else. In the matter of school standards, Washington politicos are much more interested in hearing from Lou Gerstner than from the executive director of NCTE, never mind a teacher from Walla Walla.

Politico chicanery aside, the NCTE/IRA document ends up enraging many while informing few. Take the way it addresses the teaching of standard English. Three standards relate to this topic:

Standard 4: Students adjust their use of spoken, written, and visual language (e.g., conventions, style, vocabulary) to communicate effectively with a variety of audiences and for different purposes.

Standard 6: Students apply knowledge of language structure, language conventions (e.g., spelling and punctuation), media techniques, figurative language, genre and discuss print and non-print texts.

Standard 9: Students develop an understanding of and respect for diversity in language use, patterns, and dialects across cultures, ethnic groups, geographic regions, and social roles.

In newspapers across the country, editorial writers complained with more than a little justification that they don't know what all this means. The determined reader can find clues elsewhere in the document, but few will feel the effort is worthwhile. In a paragraph titled "Systems and Structures of Language" the document declares that "the study of language conventions, including grammar, punctuation, and spelling" to be "critical," though the reader who wonders when students might be expected to switch from invented to conventional spelling or learn, say, the niceties of capitalization, may also wonder just when students should come to "understand how language conventions vary from one context to another." The moveable verb? The comma in transition? One can see why local districts are tempted to cut to the chase and announce something idiotic like students "mastering" nouns in first grade, verbs in second, and the short story in sixth.

There is a further gloss on this point in Chapter Three: "To ensure that they can communicate effectively with a wide range of audiences, all students need to learn what we refer to as 'the language of wider communication'— the forms of our language that are most commonly recognized as standard English." If NCTE veterans who came close to shedding blood over NCTE's position statement of decades past, "The Students' Right to Their Own Language," worry that this new circumlocution signals retrenchment, a statement follows that got plenty of play in the press: "This does not imply that other varieties of English are somehow incorrect or invalid; rather it means that all students need to have standard English in their repertoire of language forms and to know when they should use it."

I am not an advocate of that subskill, kill/drill curriculum of circling nouns and verbs, but as a longtime teacher I recognize that those characteristics that experts insist on dismissing as merely surface features of language are what the public care about, items that convince them whether or not teachers are doing their job. That same public is alarmed by vague, pompous, and preachy statements about "the language of wider communication." If English teachers wanted to reassure the public, they'd promise to devise a program, say, for getting across one hundred spelling demons. I'm not making this suggestion in jest. Teachers should be proactive, not letting themselves to get forced into a defensive mode: Why not choose some small item on which to make a preemptive strike and earn ourselves a public relations coup?

I am not apologetic about the fact that as a third-grade teacher I gave weekly spelling quizzes, even though I knew they improved my students' spelling not a whit. I devised spelling quizzes that did not oppress my students but did reassure parents about my "standards." And as an unacknowledged *quid pro quo*, parents let me get away with being the only teacher in the district who did not use a basal. Not one parent complained about the fact we did not have a reading textbook in our classroom. Not one. And no administrators complained either. Maybe they knew better.

When I return to the classroom, I will prove my standards to the public by sending home a flyer the first week of school, announcing the institution of "spelling demons" training. When your real work is both ephemeral and radical, to give the public a few specific, even practical, skills by which they can be reassured that you and their children are working hard seems like good manners as well as damn good *realpolitik*. Hey, I could do worse than learn a few of those demons myself.

I am very sorry that NCTE/IRA refused to consider either the truth or the necessity of public perceptions and paranoias. Decades of professional soul-searching, debate, anguish, and argument burn beneath the surface of their document. So seemingly innocuous a phrase as "the language of wider communication" thinly covers a battlefield, its antagonists bloody but unbowed. Every page of the document contains half a dozen such phrases, phrases that conceal more than they reveal.

In one sense *Standards for the English Language Arts* takes the high road. It refuses to list the spelling demons third-graders will master; it refuses to decree in which grade students should acquire the apostrophe. Certainly it would have been a whole lot easier to follow in the footsteps of the

National Education Goals Panel, which tells us that in fourth grade a student will "employ more than basic grammar and punctuation skills in writing" as well as "have the ability to analyze and edit one's own work to make it more precise and convincing." And by eighth grade students will "know how to create complex fictional characters and how to build essay arguments." Are they nuts? I make my living as a writer and I have never created a complex fictional character in my life. And surely we must ask if the world really needs more novelists. Even when a teacher has the nutty notion of stemming the production of a kid who loves to write, it doesn't work. My own seventh-grade teacher asked me (in vain) to stop turning in so many long, unassigned papers.

The late Albert Shanker, president of the American Federation of Teachers and a great Standardisto, took this low road of establishing skill schedules. Vocal in his support of National Education Goals, Shanker was a proponent of the dangerous notion that "Unless we have standards that tell us, grade by grade, what the teacher is required to teach and the student required to learn, many of our students will not reach the level of competence that we expect of high school graduates."

Writers who refer to their school days in their memoirs refute this notion. In a poignant passage in *An Unfinished Journey*, Shiva Naipaul remarks of his brother, who was twelve years older, "The Hindu Trinidad of his youth was not the Hindu Trinidad of my youth. We did not have a shared past; we did not have a shared pool of memory, ancestral or otherwise." If Naipaul could say this of a tiny place like Trinidad, how can national standards speak to a land as large and diverse as ours? Can the children of the late 1990s be expected to continue to drag along the intellectual baggage of their great-great-great-grandparents? Might not today's children in Fresno have different needs from the children in Anchorage and the children in Nantucket? A one-size-fits-all curriculum ends up fitting nobody. To accept the Standardistos' lists and timetables is to accept a gloomy and stagnant, deterministic view of culture and of children.

NCTE/IRA's *Standards for the English Language Arts* would have gained Washington approval and become a best seller if the writers had stooped to prescribing periods and nouns to first grade, commas and verbs to second, telling first-graders to read Aesop, third-graders *Heidi*, tenth graders *Great Expectations*. Standardistos applaud the notion that the only good author is a dead one. I have serious quarrels with the NCTE/IRA Standards writers but I don't accuse them of being Standardistos, and I thank them for not trying to lead their members along the low road through the muck of skill bogs.

A CALL FOR LOWERING STANDARDS

Standardistos moan and groan that we're raising a generation of know-nothings. Although it is difficult to argue against youths knowing Sophocles, Shakespeare, and Tom Sawyer, I am prepared to do it. And I'm outraged that the list-makers don't know *The Stupids* or *Frog and Toad* or hink pinks, surely essential items in a second-grader's rite of passage. We need to remind ourselves that our students come to us with lots of information undreamt of in our own philosophies just a few years ago. For starters, my third graders knew about black holes, knew about sexual matters that would make the proverbial sailor blush, and were familiar with specific applications of the Bill of Rights, such as the *Miranda* decision.

If keepers of the canon would admit, "Here is what interests us, warts and all, now why don't you make your own list of what interests you?" I'd say, "Fine." I know that good teachers are quirky, opinionated, and strongly devoted to hobbyhorses. I know their lists would differ from mine and that our students would be better for our differences. But Standardistos don't want me making my own list. They insist that their shrink-wrapped, com-mittee-certified curriculum is better than my accumulated wisdom, not to mention my devotion to a sublime wackiness. They present their lists as emerging from careful, dispassionate research; they try to palm their lists off as important and necessary. For everybody. I tell you my lists worked this year with these individual children. And knowing you can't step into the same river twice, I don't count on their working for next year's group. Each year is a new beginning.

"Why have schools failed to fulfill their fundamental acculturative re-sponsibilities?" E.D. Hirsch, Jr., asked in *Cultural Literacy*, most definitely a "when-are-you-going-to-stop-beating-your-wife?" sort of question de-signed to stop conversation. Somebody who sets himself up as expert just ain't interested in conversation. And anybody who believes teachers have ever stopped stuffing kids full of information should try teaching third grade. One chapter in my students' science text covered igneous, sedimen-tary, and metamorphic rocks, terms I first encountered in a college geology course. In social studies, my third graders were 'spozed to learn something about Timbuktu, the industrial revolution, and how New York City plans its budget. One week into this insanity, I abandon the official social studies curriculum and we read E.B. White's *Trumpet of the Swan*. My third graders also had close encounters with Aesop and Robert Louis Stevenson, both of whom made Hirsch's cut, as well as La Fontaine, Basho, Langston Hughes, Laura Ingalls Wilder, and scores of others who, like E.B. White, did not make Hirsch's list.

When Standardistos start talking about education, the self-righteousness is laid on so thick they could saw it off in chunks and use it instead of sandbags on the levees in flood season. We anti-standards folk are ever in danger of assuming the same sanctimoniousness. That's why it is so important to tell stories about classrooms, classrooms filled with the reality of kids. Mihaly Csikszentimihalyi and his coauthors of *Talented Teenagers: The Roots of Success and Failure* (Cambridge University Press, 1993), established close contact with students, equipping high schoolers with beepers, so the research team could page these students throughout the school day, asking them what they were doing, what they were thinking about, how they were feeling. That in itself is revolutionary: University scholars asking students how they're feeling. The next thing you know, somebody will come up with the idea of asking teachers the same thing.

These researchers found that in a typical history classroom, while the teacher was, say, lecturing about Genghis Khan's invasion of China and the conquest of Beijing in 1215, only two out of twenty-seven students were thinking about anything remotely connected to China when they were beeped. One of these two was remembering a meal at a Chinese restaurant, and the other was wondering why Chinese men wore their hair in a ponytail. Nobody mentioned Genghis Khan or Beijing or 1215. Add Csikszentimihalyi to the list of people who know that just because you taught it you can't assume students learned it. Then turn to Chapter Five and read the California history standards for seventh graders.

Probably it's too much for Standardistos to grasp how rare it is for students to learn what we teach, but the hallucinatory nature of Standardistos' rhetoric serves no one but them and their publisher cronies. In a conversation with Bill Moyers on the PBS Television series *The Language of Life*, the poet Robert Bly told this wonderful story about William Stafford:

> A man once asked Bill, "Is it true you write a poem every day?" Bill answered, "Yes." Then the man asked, "Well, what if you're not so good that day?" And Bill said, "I just lower my standards."

Robert Bly concluded, "That's the most helpful thing said about poetry in forty years!" It's a wonderfully useful concept for education, too. New York

State Standardistos fantasize about six-hour-long reading and writing proficiency tests as well as tests in foreign language and calculus; in Massachusetts, Standardistos insist that students will prove they're worthy of a high school diploma by reading *Moby Dick*; in Illinois, there's a call for kids to explain the fusion process in stars if they want to get out of ninth grade. Who's kidding whom? It's definitely time for a lowering of standards.

4

The Baseball/Medical Metaphors that Rule and Ruin Education

ELIMINATING DEVIATION PART I

On March 31, 1998, 48,500 fans in Phoenix welcomed the Arizona Diamondbacks, baseball's newest expansion team. In *Big League, Big Time* (Pocket, 1998), Len Sherman gives us an inside view of the standards that rule the game. Standards for players are spelled out in a manual that explains and defines in detail "every move and thought, so there would be no doubt and no deviation." Here are the directions for all Diamond back shortstops about where to stand in the infield:

1. Basic—Eight strides from 2nd base and sixteen strides deep of the line.

2. D.P. Depth—Walk in four strides and move two strides closer to the base in the double play situation.

3. Sacrifice Bunt

   a. Runner on First—Move in as the hitter shows bunt. Do not move to the base until the ball is bunted.

   b. Runner on Second (or first and second)—Hold the runner on second base in the normal fashion. See shortstop fundamentals.

And so on. All teams have these manuals. *The New York Yankees Player Development Manual,* for example, spells out when a player should dive for the ball:
Dive at tough balls in these situations:

a. Runner at 2nd base—2 outs.

b. Runner at 3rd base—2 outs.

All this seems obvious to the point of being ridiculous. It seems incredible that someone playing in the outfield at Yankee Stadium, where Joe DiMaggio and Mickey Mantle once stood, would need to be told to try really hard to catch "balls which are hit softly into the outfield and can possibly be caught."

Diamondbacks manager Tommy Jones explained to Sherman that many of today's ballplayers received "lousy instruction" in high school and college with the result that they lack "a solid grasp of the fundamentals." Somehow, this sounds suspiciously familiar. Bad enough the schools have stopped teaching the ABC's; they don't even teach how to catch a ball.

Jones is a Standardistos' Standardisto, insisting that baseball players become great by hearing instructions for the basic routines repeated over and over and over. "Always say the same thing, the same way." When the political pendulum swings and Bill Honig and Barbara Foorman and their Standardisto cronies are forced to look for honest work, they should consider getting themselves a baseball franchise. I understand Sacramento is looking for one. And this duo already knows the ritual: Always say the same thing, the same way. Over and over and over.

ELIMINATING DEVIATION PART II

At a Reading Summit held in Illinois in August of 1996, University of Houston professor Barbara Foorman didn't discuss baseball, but she did push repetition of basic routines. Foorman said that children at risk for reading disability do best when their teachers present "highly structured, intense programs that explicitly teach application of phonologic rules to print." Foorman presented unpublished data (which has since been disputed and revised: See Denny Taylor's *Beginning to Read and The Spin Doctors of Science* (NCTE, 1998)) comparing the achievement of three groups of children: Those receiving direct instruction, embedded phonics, and whole language.

An educator in the audience asked, "Isn't it difficult to control a teacher's methodology? What about a teacher's individual style? Don't most teachers look at everything and then integrate the elements from various approaches that work for them? Aren't most teachers eclectic?"

Foorman replied, "We had careful monitoring of the teachers. First there was thirty hours of training during the summer. Then every teacher was monitored in the classroom every other week—or every day, if necessary. We were breathing down the necks both of raw recruits and veteran teachers." Foorman continued, "The teacher variable does not contribute significantly above and beyond the curriculum, so what we have here is a powerful mathematical model. My hypothesis is that the teacher variable will be even less significant within the direct instruction group."

This is a numbing pronouncement. I was there; I know she said it. Foorman is insisting, first, that children are best served when teachers are subservient to technique, and second, that teachers don't matter. This tenet cuts to the core of the Standardistos argument: Choose the right technique/text/ program and any teacher can deliver it. Call me paranoid, but isn't the next step reducing costs by getting an aide to deliver the material? Then they can eliminate the aide and let the machines do it. If content, what we teach, is the only thing that matters, then this makes sense. Never mind that we've been there/done that. Strong on textbook histories, Standardistos have no clue about the histories and traditions of the schoolhouse.

I remember the year when remedial reading teachers in my district were ordered to color code all the workbooks and other ersatz reading materials to match the newly-purchased computerized behavioral checklists—so reading could be delivered on schedule. Fifteen minutes after this insanity started, I skipped out of remedial reading and set up a storefront school for kids the high school was desperate to exclude from the regular campus. Following e.e. cummings' advice, I requested an interview with the superintendent and politely told him "there's some shit I won't eat." So he put me in charge of Jack and thirty-nine other young punks.

Surely Foorman's words make Frederick Winslow Taylor, the first efficiency expert, the man who undertook a lifelong quest for finding "the one best way" to do things, dance in his grave. It was Taylor, after all, who declared that the control of work must be taken from the workers and placed in the hands of planners and thinkers. Workmen—elements of production to be studied, manipulated, and controlled—were to do as they were told. As Taylor wrote early in this century in *Shop Management*, "Each man must learn how to give up his own particular way of doing things, adapt his methods to the many new standards, and grow accustomed to receiving and obeying directions covering details, large and small, which in the past have been left to his judgment." Adapting our methods to the many new standards. . . . obeying directions. Now, where have we heard this recently?

Emily Dickinson wrote of feeling "zero at the bone" when she met a snake. Sitting in that Illinois reading summit, hearing about what was going on in Houston and California classrooms, I knew that feeling. The goal is clearly stated: Get rid of teacher variability. Put out a manual that tells the undifferentiated work force exactly what to do to their undifferentiated students. *Eight strides from 2nd base and sixteen strides deep of the line.*

Finding the "right" sequence of skill presentation is at the heart of the California standards treadmills, running their continuous loop night and day, grinding out edicts on teacher behavior. For conspiracy theorists, I would point out that former California Superintendent of Public Instruction and present teacher training entrepreneur Bill Honig was sitting at Barbara Foorman's side, and when a teacher in the audience complained that "yours is a very narrow definition of reading," Honig jumped up, grabbed the microphone, and said, "Automatic fluent decoding is the key. This data correlates with comprehension under any definition of reading down the road. It is not legitimate criticism to say this is too narrow a definition of reading." Honig's enterprise, the Coalition on Reading (CORE), has gained the official approval of the current State Board of Education to deliver staff development to California districts, an approval denied to independent professors and teachers throughout the country. I admit I lost exact count, but over the two-day conference, Honig jumped up about forty-eight times to intone that "automatic fluent decoding is the only definition of reading that counts." Honig offers proof of Blaise Pascal's contention that most of the evils of life arise from man's being unable to sit still in a room.

Another audience member asked, "It looks like you're saying that we shouldn't spend money on staff development. All we need to do is buy the right program."

Foorman replied, "Teachers need training in the context of demonstrably effective programs. Some teachers were 'visited' more than others." Turn to Chapter Five for a gloss on what "training in the context of demonstrably effective programs" means.

AND GOD SAID, "LET THERE BE PHONEMIC AWARENESS."

Proponents of systematic, explicit, direct phonics present their skill drill advocacy under the guise of a Phonics Reclamation Program, rather like the Endangered Species Act. They claim that whole language adventurists killed off phonics. Honig, for one, talks as though phonics were driven into hiding when teachers misunderstood his efforts as state superintendent to bring good literature into the classroom. All he's trying to do now is get those phonemes back. I hear the theme song from "Rawhide" in my inner ear. Round up the schwas, hog-tie them, don't let any escape. Rawhide. Whipcrack.

The absurdity of this contention is that, as vocal as whole language teachers are, they have never represented more than ten percent of the teacher total. If reading scores plummeted in California, investigators might look at California policy makers' decision to eliminate libraries and librarians and to make primary grade class size among the largest in the nation rather than to the practices of a small number of whole language teachers. As National-Louis University Professor Donna Ogle pointed out at the Illinois Reading Summit, "We don't have a state where teachers haven't been teaching phonics. We're also concerned that kids in eighth and tenth grades who have come through very traditional reading programs are at most risk and are the ones whose scores are declining the most in terms of the IGAP test."

Most people who are opposed to hard-core phonics are opposed to the hard-core part, not the phoneme part. What is distressing is that when state officials decree lock-step curriculums for teachers to teach and children to learn, children are doomed to recurring instruction of crises, and there's never any time in the school day for them to experience the joys of literature. So we have children who aren't being read to at home not being read to at school either.

USC professor Stephen Krashen warns against such a crisis curriculum, the overemphasis on "early intervention," pointing out that although "all children may go through a fairly similar developmental path in language, literacy, and cognitive development, they do not go through this path at the same rate" (*Every Person a Reader: An Alternative to the California Task Force Report on Reading*, 1996). Krashen points out that rather than focusing on getting all kindergartners on grade level, whatever that could mean, we should concentrate on getting kids to read a lot. More particularly, we should encourage them to read what they like to read. That is a revolutionary notion that few schools have tried. Standing back and letting the kids read. New York State University professor Richard Allington has been pleading for decades for schools to let the kids read. Neither Krashen nor Allington is listed as a resource in *The Little Red Reading Book: Research on*

Reading Instruction, published by the Illinois State Board of Education. Standardistos quote other Standardistos.

LOOKING FOR STUDENTS
WHO LOOK LIKE US

In *The Rise and Fall of English* (Yale, 1998), Brown professor Robert Scholes talks of "service courses," which "like the service entrances of mansions, are for those benighted folk who are not permitted to use the front door." Scholes observes that we in education distinguish sharply, and on a bias very close to social class, between those who seek to become like us and those with whom we must deal as lesser breeds. So we decree that we'll get every sixth grader reading Shakespeare and every eighth grader taking algebra, not because it makes any sense for the kids but because these are the kinds of people we want to teach. And forcing the traditional canon into ever lower grades is easier than figuring out significant alternatives. You can tell me your third graders read Chaucer and I'll take your word for it. But don't expect bouquets. Just because you can train children to do something doesn't mean they should be doing it. You tell me all your eighth graders are reading Chaucer or Shakespeare or Homer or Dickens and I'll tell you how heavy my heart is. I remember what happened when a first grader of exceptional reading ability was sent to the library to do a research assignment. Marilynn Peterson, a librarian extraordinaire, set him up with a pre-cyclopedia, a sort of encyclopedia with training wheels. Fifteen minutes later, noticing that he wasn't reading, Marilynn asked, "Do you understand how to do it?"

The boy stared at her very solemnly, "You know, just because I *can* read doesn't mean I want to read all that." Marilynn put away the pre-cyclopedia and introduced the exceptional reader to riddle books. Always, always, we must consider the children, remembering that each one of them is more important than any speeded-up notion of excellence.

Because I taught in a district that never saw a government grant it wouldn't grab, and because I like to try new things, I have taught everything from high school English to first grade remedial reading, with K-6 science, ninth-grade honors, third-grade rotten readers, and high school dropouts in-between. Because of this variety of teaching posts, I taught Distar to a boy named Keith in first grade (Yes, Distar, now reborn as SRA Mastery Reading); I also tried to teach him real reading in fourth grade and again in seventh and eighth.

Keith received extensive Distar training from his first grade teacher. I was the designated coach, providing an extra session to children identified as being at "supreme risk." I was so distressed by these Distar kids thinking what we were doing was reading that I insisted I had to see them a second time during the day. So we had lunch together. They ate and I read aloud to them. I taught them all to "read" a book of their choice. Phonics Phreaks go nuts at the notion of giving kids books like the Dr. Seuss *Hat Book* because the picture clues help kids guess at such words as "too pointy/too curly." But those kids, bombarded with ugly little worksheets, were thrilled to "read" a real book. They traveled the school hallways demonstrating their achievement to the principal and to fellow students.

Today we'd call Keith attention deficit disordered. Then, we called him trouble. Most of the time Keith was willing to listen to me read, but if I tried to offer him a book, he'd run away. Literally. So I removed this pressure from our lunchtime gatherings. I brought in hammers and nails and boards. I read aloud for half the lunch period, and the kids pounded for the other half. So those children went through first grade thinking reading was a combination of performance art and pounding on boards. Better than their thinking reading is only disjointed nonsense syllables. Keith and I both learned something important: We learned he *could* stand still and concentrate when he wanted something as badly as he wanted to be able to hit that nail.

REMEDIAL READING BY ANOTHER NAME

Knowing that I could never be an accessory to Distar again, at the end of the year I changed schools. But Keith stayed on. I met up with him again in fourth grade. He came to my science center, where I'd used a stack of Elementary Science Study teacher guides, which were at once elliptical and profound, to transform a remedial reading room into a hands-on science center where rotten readers wanted to be.

Like many kids, Keith liked to work the room, checking on what everybody else was doing. The miracle of such a room is that kids don't just "do" their own project; they pretty much do everybody else's too. So although Keith might have chosen a month-long chemistry project, he also got an eyeful of bones, pendulums, ice cube melting rates, the physics of sound (which culminated in the construction of a Clorox bottle guitar. The district language arts coordinator never set foot in the room, but the music coordinator found money to buy all the lumber, screw eyes, and fishing line. He also gave me discarded trumpets and French horns, so we had a parade whenever the spirit moved us.). Keith wandered more than most, but he also followed the rules of the room: Make a choice and do at least six experiments before changing topics, and submit a written report after each session. Although he did not read, Keith did produce phonics-based sentences. He liked helping first graders write their reports.

FAKING READING

Keith, of course, *said* he read. By the time I met him again in seventh grade, Keith had spent ten years in elementary school pretending to read. In seventh grade alone, Keith bluffed his way through a three-year-stack of *National Geographics*, biographies of George Washington, Davy Crockett, Frederic Douglass, and Babe Ruth. Plus a complete set of encyclopedias.

"You're going to read what?" I sputtered the day Keith announced with a perfectly straight face that he was going to read the encyclopedias.

"A to Z," Keith explained, waving an encyclopedia. Maybe he wanted to prove to me he'd been around the block a few times with encyclopedias. More likely, he probably figured I didn't know and he'd better explain it to me. One of the basic rules of schools is that teachers who teach smart kids, the students, say, enrolled in advanced placement classes, must be smart. Teachers who teach remedial classes must be dumb. No one is more convinced of this fact than them remedial readers.

The encyclopedias in our classroom were one of two junior sets. No official would believe that a middle school library needed easy-read books, so media expert and kid-watcher Gail VanValkenburg shut down the library, went to a closing elementary school, and dragged boxes of books to her car. The library in our new, multi-million dollar school housing urban seventh and eighth graders was afflicted with Standards. No picture books, no easy-read books, no riddle books. My idea of a joke was to send a student down to the library to check out *Absolom! Absolom!* or *Autocrat of the Breakfast Table* for me. Even I couldn't bring myself to check out any of the three biographies of Oliver Cromwell.

THE HOBGOBLIN OF LITTLE MINDS

Keith had a predictable repertoire: Throwing spitwads, insisting he was bleeding internally and had to be examined by the nurse or the paramedics, making obscene noises, removing screws from the bookshelves. Keith was an expert in screw removal. Exhibiting considerable subtlety, he'd perfected the practice to an art form, managing to arrange things so that when someone else touched the shelves and sixty-three books crashed to the floor with a satisfying clatter, he was on the other side of the room, ready to launch into his dramatic *Who me?* performance of aggrieved innocence if I dared to question him.

For two periods a day while Keith was in seventh and eighth grades, I vacillated between trying to ignore him and threatening his well-being if he dared to get out of his chair one more time or made one more ugly sound. The "Be consistent" advice offered to fledgling parents and teachers alike waves a false banner of hope for producing the smoothed-out, standard-issue kids we think we want. Behavior modification programs marketed under the slogan of classroom control train teachers to establish a hierarchy of classroom infractions along with corresponding demerit checks and what is known in the lingo of our trade as "consequences." The flip side of meting out consequences is, of course, giving out gold stars and other fribble as a reward for compliance. I worry about such systems because I think they clog up and confuse a student's ethical development. When a teacher runs her classroom by a system of punishments and rewards, the student is encouraged to become a passive recipient of her control. Read Alfie Kohn's *Punished by Rewards* (Houghton Mifflin, 1995) and *Beyond Discipline* (Association for Supervision & Curriculum Development, 1996) and you will have a hard time ever giving out gold stars again.

Passivity can't breed responsibility, and here we come to the connection with reading. A daily ritual of phoneme injection breeds passivity, never singing for children. And children who haven't heard words sing, who have not experienced words that make them laugh and cry, words that make them stomp and holler and words that make them go suddenly quiet, even pensive, are not going to be readers, no matter how adept they are at decoding. Just as I want students who behave even when I'm not looking, I also want them to pick up a book when I'm not looking. And you're only tempted to pick up a book when you think there might be something in it for you.

Emerson was definitely on to something when he called consistency "the hobgoblin of little minds," but Aldous Huxley went even further, insisting, "The only completely consistent people are the dead." And there it is: The grave is a quiet place, a consistent place, a place for standards. Everywhere else, we must expect the hurly-burly, and, considering the alternative, even thank our stars for it. Of course a teacher must try to be fair, but the consistency of seven-step lesson plans or phonemes all lined up in a row and demerit checklists with uniform consequences is cheap veneer, rather like throwing a giant tarp over a bog of quicksand.

When a teacher hasn't a clue of what else to do, she can strive to be consistent, to react to each student according to the manual of established rules published by some committee sitting in a distant corporate tower. She'd do better to throw a two-minute snit and be done with it. Kids need a living, breathing person who reacts to classroom moments with judgment, compassion, quirkiness, and yes, even an occasional snit or two.

One of the best things I ever did as a third-grade teacher was to spot one of Beatrix Potter's tiny *Peter Rabbit* volumes in the window of a news-stand while I was waiting for the bus to school. Amazingly, I had never read Potter. On the spur of the moment I bought that book, and I rushed into class, saying to the kids, "Look what I have!" They were intrigued by the size, and they fell in love with Peter. So the next morning I bought another one. And another. As they say, "The rest was history." Rotten reader Tom ended up copying out all of *Peter* by hand because "I just like the feel of the words." For a couple of weeks Chris piled eleven little Potter books on his desk while he read something else during our hour of silent reading because "I like them nearby." Jenny asked me for Beatrix Potter's address so she could write her, telling her how much she loved the books. When I told Jenny that Beatrix Potter was dead, she went away for a while, very pensive. Later she asked me if Beatrix Potter had any kids she could write to. The android pro-grammed to deliver Mastery Reading doesn't have time to build such literary history in her classroom, not if she has storm troopers conducting inspec-tion tours, anyway.

State boards of education, corporate chiefs, and politicians offer paltry fare for the classroom, not realizing that the best thing a teacher has to offer is herself. This principle is hard, not easy. It means that in the end we have no plans, no procedures, no theories, no checklists to hide behind. It is a very dangerous notion to tell a teacher that the right reading program or the right set of standards is enough. The manual hasn't been written that can tell someone how to teach a class of third graders. After we read everything we can get our hands on, after we study and travel to conferences and work hard to become smart in our profession, the best moments in our classrooms come from impulse, not from carefully constructed plans. This is why I am so skeptical about national teaching standards. How do you test for a sense of humor? A good heart? A generous spirit? A tolerance for ambiguity? An ability to step in at the right moment as well as the ability to step back and take the long pause? Standardistos seem to tell us that competence is enough. Garrison Keillor observes, "Love brings people to safety when com-petence can go no further." Where's the test for love?

It was instinct rather than affection that kicked in on the day when Keith's whining insistence that he'd read every single book in our classroom had reduced my patience to the consistency of warm Jell-O. I grabbed *Hop on Pop* and shoved it at him. "Read this!" I commanded in a voice he recognized as non-negotiable. I walked away and Keith started turning the pages quickly, his method of reading all books. But then something caught his eye. He stopped and looked at a page, really looked. Then he went back to the preceding page and examined it closely. Keith stared at that page for a long time. Then he turned to the first page and started mouthing words.

As he hunched over that book sounding out the words, Keith did not move for the rest of the period. Other kids picked up on the enfolding drama and, unusual for this group of seventh- and eighth-grade roughnecks, remained silent in the face of a miracle: Keith was reading a book. I am not exaggerating when I say the rest of us presented a frozen tableau rather like that old game of "Statues" while Keith, oblivious to the outside world, concentrated on his book.

When Keith finally looked up from the book, his expression was puzzled. "I did it. I *read* this book," he said. He looked at me. "Seriously, Miz O. I read it. For real. I read this book. You wanna see?" It wasn't fluent reading. Each word was pointed at, struggled over, sounded out. Then, Keith made the leap that had been missing for all those remedial reading years. After sounding out a word, he pronounced it as a sense-making word, not just a sound. Keith was fifteen years old and this was one of the easiest of the Dr. Seuss books—not near the level of sophistication of, say, *Cat in the Hat*. Nonetheless, it was a magical moment for Keith and for me. No matter what happens to Keith in the future, nobody can ever say he hasn't read a book. I've lived in three different states since that day, carrying that tattered copy of *Hop on Pop* with me. Today, I look at it and I wish I'd given it to Keith, but at the time he didn't ask for it and I clung to it as my red, white, and blue badge of courage. The boy who had tried my patience and my ingenuity for so many years had finally read a book.

Whenever things weren't going well for Keith during the rest of the year, he'd say to me, "Say, how would you like to hear that *Hop on Pop* book?" and he'd pull up a chair and calm himself by reading a few pages out loud. Like everyone who has liked *The Son of Sinbad* or *The Black Stallion Returns* or *Little Men* or *Star Trek LVII*, Keith knew what he liked. "Did that Dr. Seuss write any more books?" he asked. I thought of the administrative constraints that would not pay for my requested subscription to the book club for beginning readers. So I joined on my own. Think about Keith as you read the California history standards in Chapter Five.

Principals and curriculum coordinators have Standards edicts, world class competitions, grade level guidelines, and checklists to keep, and miles to go before they sleep. School districts establish purchasing procedures, making it almost impossible for a teacher to exercise her savvy about kids and books. My district would readily purchase any number of glitzy $500 phonics kits that I might request—or $5,000 worth of texts and tapes and charts labeled *complete reading program*. They feel comfortable buying workbooks and flashcards and other tiddly-pom labeled *skill development*. Plus, of course, the computer paraphernalia labeled *reading accountability system* to go along with it. But I couldn't get Dr. Seuss, a subscription to the local newspaper, or five copies of a Farley Mowat story about his life with wolves unless I paid for them myself.

WHEN THE BLAMELESS MEETS THE BONEHEAD

Keith's history in our school system is both typical and complex. Keith was very slow, very frustrated, and more than a little off-center personality-wise. I believed his oddness stemmed in large part from his years of struggle to make some sense of the impossible curriculum the school district offered in the name of mainstreaming: The farce called equal educational opportunity for all. In his regular seventh grade academic classes, Keith was expected to read textbooks and pass tests on the Dutch colonial plans in the New World, to define the functions of the human body (see example p. 84), to figure the interest rates on home mortgages. One of my definitions of obscenity is insisting that kids living in crumbling federally-administered projects learn how to figure home interest rates. I wonder how most school board members, administrators, and people who sit on committees drafting academic standards would behave if they were forced to sit, say, in graduate physics classes for six hours a day, five days a week. They'd get twenty-seven minutes for lunch but no coffee breaks or other recesses. For some comic relief they could take showers together after gym.

Keith passed seventh grade both because we worried about having a 15-year-old in seventh grade and because even the most hard-line Standardisto among us knew holding Keith back would do no good. Keith had already been held back twice in his school career. I'm being realistic, not cynical, when I say that Keith could have spent ten years in seventh grade and he still wasn't going to understand the Dutch sea routes or how blood circulates in the body. Standardistos can talk until the cows come home about establishing benchmarks and gates and hurdles and moats so that a kid can't get to seventh grade without being able to read. I just want to know what they're going to do with all the fifteen-year-olds stranded in second grade. Nobody who has taught for more than sixty-eight minutes believes that everybody can learn everything. The sad part is that when kids like Keith are taught everything, they don't end up learning much of anything.

Pass or fail, Keith was, of course, still my student in eighth grade. And he didn't cause much havoc during eighth grade. When I mentioned to the principal that Keith seemed to be wandering the halls a lot, he told me not to worry, that he was aware of Keith's wandering, but since Keith was not a malicious or destructive boy, he allowed it. "Keith has his uses," he explained. What he meant was that he was cultivating Keith to be the school's number one stool pigeon. Keith couldn't recite the Gettysburg Address or define an alluvial whatever, but, by God, the boy was on top of everything happening in the school hallways. Especially if it wasn't supposed to be happening.

From first grade on, there's always a kid who knows the system at its most basic level. If I needed, say, a mop or a screwdriver or an extension cord from the custodian, I consulted Keith, who knew both where the custodian was at any given moment and also where the needed item was. "Mrs. Smith has the screwdriver, but she's done with it. I'll get it."

Keith could tell administrators who wrote the dirty word on the lavatory walls, who was sneaking a smoke behind the gym, who had pot in his locker. Keith was extremely proud of this role. He explained to me that the principal both needed and depended on him. I feared this role was destined for disaster, but Keith and the principal, who had similar hyperactive personalities, had formed a bond they both enjoyed.

Although my partner and I coached students for their academic classes, we abandoned this practice for Keith when he entered eighth grade. We looked at his social studies curriculum—trace the causes of World War I, explain the differences between socialism, communism, and democracy—and decided that Keith should stick with Dr. Seuss. After the Seuss breakthrough, Keith actually read a number of simple books. Once I decided to forget the other curriculum, I felt less pressure, and so did Keith. His behavior improved and he began to work harder at reading. And once he became the principal's *aide de camp*, his academic teachers didn't feel pressured to keep him in class. Everybody relaxed. I guess we knew it wasn't right, but we relaxed anyway. I would ask the Standardisto militia: What are you supposed to do when you have a whacko kid, whacko curriculum requirements, and a wacko principal whose only academic mission is wreaking justice on kids who write dirty words on the lavatory walls?

So Keith came to the end of eighth grade on somewhat of an upbeat note, another year of perfect attendance and more than a dozen books under his belt. Of course Keith didn't pass his final exams, but because he was nearly sixteen, he was routed on to the high school as a matter of course. Keith was very proud of the suit his mother had bought him for graduation.

Then the axe fell. Two days before the graduation ceremony, the administrators decided that since he had not passed his final exams, Keith could not attend the graduation ceremony. "We have to maintain standards," they intoned. "Graduation off the stage should be reserved for those who have earned it." I guess in another, more perfect world, I might support such a principle, but I don't think you can change the rules two days before graduation. A hurried exception was made for special education students, the kids who were "mainstreamed into academic classes for purposes of socialization." I argued that Keith had been recommended for special education status as far back as third grade and that it was only because of quite incredible school district snafus that he had not been declared exempt from those final exams.

Ironically, my classes were depended on to mainstream in reverse; we were invited to all fetes put on by the Downs Syndrome class. We were invited because we could be relied upon to be a polite, even enthusiastic, audience. I can't think of a skill in which I put higher value than learning kindness. I'm not talking of some paltry thing, as my former school district puts it in its whacko language arts standards, *mastering etiquette*; I'm talking about the ability to put yourself in someone else's shoes, the ability to reach out to people and touch their lives, the ability to care for them. Some of my students had reputations for being the nastiest troublemakers in the school, but they were staunch allies of the Downs Syndrome group. Keith, who didn't exhibit much self-awareness or ability to socialize with his own classmates, always volunteered for opportunities to work with "the gang," as he liked to call them. The gang was as enthusiastic about Keith as he was about them. They never failed to exchange high-fives in the hallways, and the day he walked into their classroom to read *Hop on Pop*, he walked seven feet tall.

But it's easier for Standardistos to show sympathy for a Downs Syndrome child than for a child like Keith. The principal, Keith's buddy all year, suddenly wanted to be an educational leader, a setter of academic standards. He insisted that Keith didn't even try. Evidence of this was the fact that he cut so many classes.

I phoned the assistant superintendent in charge of curriculum, who was also in charge of graduation policy. I explained that Keith's records documented a district oversight in not following up on a psychological services recommendation to place him in special class in fourth grade. I explained that his tested IQ was 70, that he was not capable of doing the work demanded from his academic classes, and that no alternative assignments had been made available to him.

"I appreciate your input," said the assistant superintendent in charge of curriculum. "But the principal has informed me that this boy continually cut classes and wandered the halls. We cannot condone or reward this type of behavior."

"He was never in any serious trouble," I pleaded. "He didn't cut classes, not really. He thought he had been appointed special agent of the principal to keep an eye out for troublemakers and to report their misdeeds." I choked on my tears, and I knew that this woman who had been my nemesis for so many years knew I was crying.

"I've made my decision," announced the voice of this person who was in charge but had not set foot in our school during the two years Keith had been there. "It is time we showed students that we have standards," she said, ending the conversation. And that was that. I wonder if Keith ever realized that stool pigeons are discarded as soon as they are of no further use. I wonder if he ever wore his new suit.

Twenty years later, as I look back on my time with Keith and reflect on what happened to him, I realize that the story is more shocking, more obscene, than I realized at the time. Keith was just one of my students, and I had lots of other desperate kids to worry over. But now, in examining the details, in relating the institutional disregard for Keith's needs and his rights, I wonder that I could keep going about my daily rounds. I wonder how I could have stayed relatively calm and relatively polite (the longest period of time during which that principal and I did not speak was seven months, and that was over toilet paper, not Keith), working with people who so carelessly disregarded the needs of children. I wonder how I could have cooperated with them on the rest of school life's minutiae. My only guess is that in order to survive teachers push a lot of ugliness to the back of their consciousness. This is why it has taken me two decades to write about Keith.

MEDICAL MAYHEM

Bill Honig is one of many who say that education should be scientific, adopting a medical model. He's wrong. Teachers who try to emulate doctors, trying to maintain an image of the all-knowing practitioner, making diagnoses and handing out prescriptions, are mostly blowing hot air. When people start blowing this air in the name of teaching, we need to consider the fact that every year ninety thousand patients in the U.S. die of a hospital-acquired infection. They go into the hospital to be treated for one thing—and whether or not that's cured, the hospital kills them.

One of the problems is that hospitals breed bugs. Even penicillin's discoverer Alexander Fleming issued a cautionary note, warning that the misuse of the drug could lead to the propagation of mutant forms of resistant bacteria. A bit more than fifty years later, the American habit of over-medicating has led to the development of "super bugs." In *The New York Times Magazine* (August 2, 1998), Sheryl Gay Stolberg reported that 25 to 45 percent of the 190 million doses of antibiotics administered even in hospitals are unnecessary, never mind those administered out of physicians' offices. Stolberg pointed out that in 1995, methicillin-resistant staph infections killed 1,409 people in New York City. That is 200 more people than were murdered in the city during the same year.

Although I believe that schools induce bugs as pernicious in their own way as those in hospitals, I don't want to carry this metaphor too far. But I do insist that we should not look at children as a disease that we need to cure. Honig is advocating this same overdosing that responsible medical experts warn against: Give every kindergartner a heavy dose of phonemic awareness, give every first and second grader an even heavier dose of systematic, explicit phonics. Systematic, explicit phonics is not new. We've been there and we've done that. The results are lots of kids who think they hate reading, kids like Keith who are super resistant to books.

People who employ medical metaphors in education emulate the cancer researchers, talking about wars and battles. Competing interest groups jostle for preeminence, not to mention money. They play on public fears. Cancer research and reading research both offer big money to the winners. The kids and the patients are not winners. In *Cancer Wars: How Politics Shapes What We Know & Don't Know About Cancer*, (Basic Books, 1995), Robert Proctor observes that, strange as it may seem, researchers can't even reach a consensus on whether cancer rates are going up or down, whether to utilize animal studies, bacterial bioassays, or longer-term epidemiological studies. Cancer researchers are more bitterly divided than reading researchers ever thought of being, probably because the financial stakes are so much higher.

Proctor asks the big questions about cancer research: Why do we know what we know, and why don't know what we don't know? Who gains from knowledge (or ignorance!) of a particular sort, and who loses? Who does science and who gets science done to them? We must ask the same questions of the materials and methods we are being told to bring to children: Why do we know what we know, and why don't we know what we don't know? Who gains from knowledge (or ignorance!) Most important, who loses?

That said, my day-to-day, working quarrel with using the medical metaphor in teaching is more folksy. Doctors deal with hematocrits and platelet counts; teachers need to deal with feelings. We are a helping, a nurturing profession. In *Life Support*, (Little, Brown, 1997) Suzanne Gordon profiles "on the front lines" nurses. Oncology nurse Nancy Rumplik talks about the "skill of involvement" and the "enervating emotional work" that is her job. Nursing scholar Patricia Benner talks about "skilled intuition," a wonderful term that I would gladly borrow for teaching.

Clinical nurse specialist Jeannie Chaisson observes that a critical aspect of nursing work goes undocumented and unrecorded. "We don't write down in the chart, 'Well, I thought the patient was possibly worried and so I sat and talked with him for half an hour.'" She adds that this talk might be more important than the record of his blood pressure and EKG. "Nursing is not a matter of reading machines and coming up with the right numbers," she insists.

Similarly, we must resist the thugs who would turn the teaching of reading into a numbers game. But when the bookkeepers want numbers, we should be ready with our numbers: How many library books do your students read in class? How many do they take home? How many minutes do you read aloud each day? From how many genres do you read aloud? How many minutes a day do your students read silently? How many minutes a day do children participate in group reading, book discussion groups, and so on? Send group totals home: *We read 780 pages (or whatever) this week!*

In my class, many kids counted letters. One of my most persistent classroom practices was to exchange daily letters with my students. Both my letter and the student's response were written in a little spiral bound notebook, so that all the letters were always available. Third graders especially liked to count their letters and express amazement. The counter would write, "Dear Mrs. O, This is my 83rd letter to you!!!!!" The counter felt a real sense of accomplishment, and so did I. Eighty-three times we had made an important connection with our words.

The textbooks used in schools are the products of committee compromises; they are books that no one outside the schoolhouse would dream of reading. But when a teacher chooses to chart her own course, choose her own books, she has to make sure she has prepared herself to do it. She'd better be sure she can make better choices than the textbook committees. Since wisdom and joy in the classroom begin with the teacher's reading aloud, that's where the first important choices are made. I decided early on that being atuned to my students interests doesn't mean I have to read the *Barf-o-Rama* series out loud. It means I said to third graders, "No, I'm sorry, but I'm not going to read *My Little Pony* book you got for Christmas to the class. I discovered at the end of my first year teaching third grade that a number of parents were reading the same chapter book aloud to their kids at home that I was reading aloud during the day. So, Dick, for example, heard Farley Mowat's *Owls in the Family* at school and again at home. His mom reported that he loved hearing it twice. When we'd finish a book at school, there would be talk at home, "What do you think she'll choose next?" I have since learned that this happens a lot. Teachers are bringing good books not just to single children but to whole families. This makes it all the more important to keep our classrooms and our lessons filled with these books. Likewise, a teacher need not hesitate about expelling Beanie Baby acquisition stories from Show and Tell. This is called Professionalism in Action. Second graders readily accept the substitution of Embarrassing Vomit Stories.

The one-time nursing model of care and comfort, of course, is something of a relic, replaced by the corporate invention of managed care that transformed the primary nursing model of bedside care into a model of profit maximization. Cost-cutting shoves caring out the back door. Staffing is cut and the remaining nurses have to deliver their goods at a UPS rate. While registered nurse positions were routinely downsized in 1994, the salaries of CEOs for the top seven for-profit HMOs averaged seven million dollars. Hospitals routinely use paraprofessionals to perform tasks formerly done by registered nurses. Anyone who can't see a similar shift coming in teaching, once schools have the "right" curriculum in place, is wearing blinders. I was present when Professor of Psychology Barbara Foorman promised Illinois education administrators and corporate chiefs that when they got the right curriculum in place, they wouldn't have to worry about teacher variability. I know, I know, I have complained about Foorman's remark eighteen times already. But I want to be sure the Standardisto intent sinks in.

I am particularly interested in the teaching-medicine parallels because hospitals in America routinely gather data on "complication rates" (things like bedsores and hospital-acquired infections and such) and death rates. This information is proprietary and rarely made public. Gordon tells the story of a patient in a San Francisco hospital who dialed 911 for help because as he lay hemorrhaging, no one in the hospital responded to his cries for assistance. What education needs is a similar 911 service for hapless students. When they go on curriculum overload, there should be an emergency number to call.

5

Californication

PAYING HOMAGE TO
NO. 38-13057400-500

Even before I started school in northern California, I knew a lot about the evil empire of the California State Department of Education and the way it quoted the rules of bureaucracy to cement its own vested interests and to block local autonomy. I grew up hearing the ugly details of just how the California State Department of Education demonstrated more interest in red tape than in feeding hungry children. Department of Education functionaries kept phoning my father, threatening to put him in jail because—and this is the truth—he had violated the official Standards of the California State Department of Education.

As president of the local board of education, Dad was very upset to hear about kids coming to school carrying a paper bag with only an onion or a raw potato for their lunch. Dad decided to do something about it. He read in the paper that disassembled portable army barracks used in the Pacific Islands during World War II were being sold cheaply. People were buying them as utility buildings, cabins, and garages. Dad thought, "Why not a cafeteria?" His fellow board members concurred.

District rules required that anything costing more than $1,000 be put out to thirty-day bid, but there was no time to wait for this process, so Dad drove 120 miles to San Francisco and bought three 24-feet by 12-feet units at $2,200 each. He borrowed the money from the bank, putting up his home and business as collateral. Then, the thirty-two crates and bundles bound by steel tape sat in our front yard while the school board followed the letter of the law and put the cafeteria out to bid. Once the legalities were satisfied, the school district paid Dad's loan at the bank and Dad enlisted local townspeople to help pour a cement slab and put the buildings together. The resulting structure most definitely wasn't pretty, but it was functional, and it soon became the center of the district's hot-lunch program, predating the federal program by decades.

Everything was fine. Every school kid ate a hot lunch every day. Then the whole deal almost blew up when high school officials contacted the State Department of Education, saying, "We want some buildings like that elementary school building." In very short order, the you-know-what hit the fan in Sacramento. "What buildings?" they demanded. And top brass promptly came to investigate. Over and over they said the same thing, "You can't do this. You can't do this." They sent architects and functionaries with rule books, people who also repeated, "You can't do this." My father was given official notification of all the codes whose requirements the ex-barracks failed to meet. Meanwhile, kids continued to eat hot lunch in their new cafeteria.

Our phone rang a lot. Dad told the State Department of Education functionaries that U.S. Government personnel had used this type of building in the Pacific Islands all through the war for whatever purposes they wanted to use them, and nobody bothered those employees. "Just because we don't belong to your association and didn't hire anybody from your approved list doesn't mean our children are going to give up their right to be fed." State functionaries told Dad if he didn't remove the nonstandard building from school district property immediately, they'd put him in jail. This sounded awfully scary to my five-year-old self, and I kept asking Dad, "Are you going to jail?" He told me if he was, it was for a good cause.

Someone at the State Department of Education finally blinked. My dad didn't go to jail, and kids ate hot lunch in that nonstandard portable barracks for thirty years or more. Actually, the school board also instituted a unique twist on busing, showing their fierce commitment to making sure no child sat in a classroom hungry. When a second elementary school was built across town, kids were bused every day to the portable barracks, fed a hot lunch, and bused back to their school. I rode that bus.

The cafeteria has since been replaced, but the building is still being used for storage. Today, Dad points out to me that although the State Department of Education blinked, he "was not invited to go out on their speakers' circuit, giving advice on how to build cheap cafeterias." While writing this book I discovered that Dad kept a souvenir of his dealings with the California State Department of Education in the garage: Nailed on a ceiling beam was a board off one of the thirty-two crates. It is labeled No. 38-13057400-500. I climbed a ladder, crowbar in hand, and pried off that board, which was solidly set with ten-penny nails. It wasn't easy, but I now am the proud owner of tangible proof of Dad's triumph over the California State Department of Education. In face of my own dismal failure to make the California State Board of Education blink, I cherish this board.

FOOL'S GOLD: http://www.cde.ca.gov

I don't know if it's the quakes, the kooks, the climate, the conspiracy theorists, or the conceit-of-the-perpetually-tanned, but California does look a bit strange to the rest of the nation. Because of statewide textbook adoptions, it also casts enormous influence over the curriculum presented to schoolchildren in the rest of the nation. These days people in the other forty-nine states need to pay special attention to what's going on with the California State Department of Education, because the California crowd is propagating and promoting a bizarre notion of what should be happening in classrooms.

In California, geographic stress infects education policy. For a Californian, nothing is less likely to occur than "average." Take California weather, for example. In the 127 years records have been kept, only seventeen percent of the years approach within twenty-five percent of the historical average. Californians experience floods or droughts; they do not experience "average." And in California, weather and water are paradigms for everything else.

These days, when you go to the California State Department of Education web site, it refers to the work of the *State of California Academic Standards Commission* as the "gold standards." I've spent a lot of time studying this material, and I call it fool's gold. The department claims to have produced K–12 standards in language arts, mathematics, science, and social studies that are "measurable and objective," reflecting "the knowledge and skills necessary for California's work force to be competitive in the global, information-based economy of the 21st century." Scorpions have sleek tongues. This sounds more like a real estate ad than educational policy. Immediately after making this promise, the California Academic Standards Commission states that these standards are "comparable in rigor to academic content and performance standards used in the school systems of America's global economic competitors" and they most definitely do *not* include "personal behavior standards or skills [such as] honesty, sociability, ethics, or self-esteem." Chapter and verse of the law forbidding standards of honesty are cited: AB 265 (Chapter 975, SB 430, Chapter 69), AB 2105, (Chapter 920, Section 60605).

I would note briefly that the oft-mentioned U.S. economic competitor insists that the most important skill it teaches has to do with personal behavior standards. In Japan, the most important thing children in grades one through six learn is how to suppress individual competition and to work for the good of the group.

In California, having world-class "gold standards" means that immigrant children are given a battery of tests—in English. On July 15, 1998, the Associated Press reported that a Fresno Unified School District teacher was suspended for five days because he refused to give a state-mandated standardized reading test, the Stanford 9, to his non-English-speaking pupils. The teacher said he thought that giving the test to second graders would have been "a humiliating insult" and ultimately harmful to them. But he must not have read Section 60605, eliminating ethics and self-esteem from his teaching imperative. New state law requires that public school students be given standardized tests (in English) in reading, language, mathematics, spelling, science, and social studies, whether the students speak English or not.

For reasons of space, I will concentrate on the language arts and history/social studies standards, but I would like to point out that the people chosen to work on academic standards in California are not unbiased. The remarkable behavior of Bill Evers illustrates this point. A participant in *Mathematically Correct*, an activist conservative group that seems to regard calculators in the hands of elementary school children as the eighth deadly sin, one of Evers' stunts was to lead a demonstration in front of the Palo Alto Unified School District building in which he flushed down a toilet California's 1992 mathematics curriculum framework. As he flushed, his co-demonstrators chanted, "Flush it. Flush it." Evers was named chair of the Academic Standards Commission subcommittee on mathematics. What qualifies Evers to be on the committee drafting mathematics standards for all schoolchildren in California? He is a political science researcher at the Hoover Institution and he heads an anti-reform group called HOLD, Honest Open Logical Debate on math reform. Go figure.

GIVE THAT HOG A FIDDLE

I have read the California Field Review of the Draft Reading/Language Arts Curriculum Framework, K–12, issued June 12, 1998; I have read the Language Arts "Challenge Standards," last uploaded January 22, 1998; I have read the California School-to-Career Framework, uploaded December 9, 1997; I have read the California Language Arts Content Standards, displayed December 1997; I have read the academic standards for Mathematics, approved December 11, 1997; I have read the academic standards for History/Social Science and Science, released in mid July-1998; I have read the minutes of sixteen full commission meetings, ranging from September 26, 1996, to May 6, 1998; I have read the minutes of six meetings of the Science Committee, minutes of nine meetings of the Reading & Writing Committee, minutes of ten meetings of the Mathematics Committee, minutes of two meetings of the History/Social Science Committee. Conspiracy theorists will want to determine why the public is kept in the dark about so many meetings of the latter group. The minutes of six meetings of the History/Social Science Committee remain sealed. Likewise, the January 8, 1997 meeting of the Full Commission has never been made public, nor has the June 3, 1998 meeting of the Science Committee. I wonder how Woodward and Bernstein got their start. I confess that sometimes in the middle of my reading I wondered if these were the minutes of an Academic Commission meeting or the rough draft of a novel by Henry James.

I have studied these documents and I acknowledge the struggles of individual committee members, acknowledge their attempt to come to grips with the complexities of the intellectual domain in question. Nonetheless, to use an old Vermont expression, these documents are about as handy as a hog with a fiddle. For those who don't have ready access to hogs, I would say that a teacher needs these documents about as much as my cat needs an electric nose hair trimmer from Sharper Image.

When we read standards with the thought of actually using them to inform our work, we must be able to distinguish chalk from cheese. However well-intentioned they may be, the Standardistos who drafted these documents offer no evidence that they possess this skill. These Standardistos are adept at lining up information. They exhibit no sensitivity toward or savvy about children. None. On May 28, 1997, Governor Pete Wilson addressed a full commission meeting, citing a meritorious Los Angeles teacher who achieves high standards with "at risk" students. Wilson offered proof of the high standards in this classroom: These sixth graders recite Shakespeare and study algebra. This kind of exhibit is the hallmark of Standardistos, cramming ever more sophisticated information into ever younger children, whether they're ready or not.

Translating educational jargon that is overlaid with political purpose into English is no fun, but somebody's got to do it. The language of the minutes of the March 11–12, 1997, meeting of the Reading & Writing Committee presages the philosophy and political purpose of the standards document they are working toward. The commissioners agree that "the K–3 standards must deliver children prepared for the kind of work described in these fourth grade models." For those who would take comfort in the fact that Pete Wilson is not their governor and because of term limits is no longer even California's governor, I would say that Pete Wilson is just a little pimple of a problem, not the real enemy. The mindset that has infected California politicians sits comfortably in just about every statehouse in the land. I would caution you to look around: California is coming.

Elsewhere in this book I discuss the "get ready" insanity that infects most of education these days. Here, I would point out that buses and obstetricians *deliver* children. I guess that teachers occasionally deliver primary graders, in the sense of getting them to line up and then walk as a group to someplace else in the building. If anybody ever sees a document deliver even one child, even for, say, the space of a centimeter, please contact me immediately. My e-mail address is on the copyright page of this book.

In April, the commissioners say: "A fifth grade teacher would have a firm grasp on what skills and knowledge had been conveyed in grades K–4, and would deliver kids to the next grade ready to continue with the next set of expectations."

Okay, the commissioners like the delivery image. But that aside, commissioners think that teachers convey skills and knowledge to children. And then they deliver the kids, skills intact, to the next grade. *Convey* is an interesting word, with its close association with *conveyance* and *conveyor*, as in *conveyor belt*. And I don't think the commissioners chose this word lightly. There is discussion throughout their meetings about the importance of choosing words carefully—so they will say what they mean and so the public will understand what they mean. This is a laudable goal and, reading all the minutes of their meetings, I was impressed that they kept coming back to language and the importance of the public's understanding what they are about.

Okay. As I'm sure every official Standardisto in California knows, the primary meaning of *convey* is to move in a continuous stream or mass, thus well suiting both the meaning and the intention of the commissioners' mission. They see knowledge as a continuous stream and students as one undifferentiated mass.

It doesn't take a conspiracy theorist to notice that the National Educational Summiteer and IBM CEO Louis Gerstner employs the same kind of language, defining education as "The distribution of information." (See Chapter Six.)

In July, the California commissioners say they want "to make a strong statement about reading broadly, sending the message that children should read independently outside of school, for vocabulary development especially, and that they should be reading for pleasure."

Giving credit where credit is due, the committee people do mention reading for pleasure. But I'm not willing to give too much credit when such a notion is mentioned only once—tacked on as an obvious afterthought. Reading for pleasure is mentioned as the instrumental, eat-your-spinach device for increasing one's vocabulary. Right. We take books to the beach, we curl up in front of the fireplace with a book, in order to increase our vocabularies. I've spent a lifetime in schools seeing proof positive that reading-as-medicine is a futile enterprise.

In contrast, USC Professor Stephen Krashen provides plenty of evidence that kids who read comic books or *Babysitters* books increase their vocabulary. I'd make an educated guess that the avid and enthusiastic readers of *Babysitters* books gain more vocabulary than if those same kids made a conscious decision to increase their vocabulary by choosing books as medicine, by choosing, say, *Gulliver's Travels* for their "pleasure reading."

There's an old saying: *Frenchmen live as if they were never to die. Englishmen die all their lives*. I want my students to read like Frenchmen. I want them to read for the pleasure their books give them today, this minute, with no thought of tomorrow. I don't want students to read as supplicants to Harvard, always with an eye out for the Standardisto lurking in the shadows with his bag of tests and measures in hand. When you condemn a kid to read for tomorrow, always conscious of improving his skills, always "getting ready," you condemn him to a slow death as a reader. In fairness, I'll let the English have the last word on this—for now. According to a sixteenth-century English proverb, *God may send a man good meat, but the devil may send an evil cook to destroy it.*

Even the good idea of "pleasure reading" is fragile under the eye of people who trust neither children nor books. Katherine Paterson, for one, decries the Standardisto postulate that children read books to increase their vocabularies. "My job is to tell a story—a story about real people who live in the world as it is." Paterson does not refer to the Standardistos by name but she does talk about "intellectual and emotional slugs." That's good enough for me.

On January 11, 1998, Commission members talk about it being their job to *raise the bar*. This kind of talk, ugly beyond comprehension, pervades the rhetoric of education terminologists throughout the land. Treating kindergartners like steeple-chase horses or pole vaulters. My niece is lucky her family ignored that raised bar when she was a kindergarten failure. Her teacher interpreted the child's failure to complete worksheets of matching sounds as an inability to complete them. A diagnosis was offered: The kid was polite but also "a daydreamer, inattentive, restless, immature." Fortunately, her family ignored the hints that such an immature and inattentive child who didn't circle rhyming phonemes might do well to repeat kindergarten. Then, in a first-grade classroom where children were encouraged to find pleasure in books of their choice, she picked up a book the first week of school and started reading. She said she could read in kindergarten, too, but "nobody ever asked me." As a high school senior, she's taking advanced placement calculus and batch of other fast-track courses that kids seem to be hurried into these days. Her dad tells me she'll be able to complete college in three years, and I wonder why anybody would want to do that.

At their February 11, 1998 meeting, the California Academic Standards Commission members decide they want to be on the "cutting edge" of performance standards, but first they have to determine what performance standards are and figure out how to develop them. Bob Dulli, the vice-president for geography education at the National Geographic Society advises the Commission that "California has more remarkable economic/political/cultural connections than the rest of the world and that the commission should take advantage of that." Remarkable statement, that. I wonder if he uses the same sales pitch when he speaks in Texas, New York, Illinois, or wherever. But Dulli, of course, is buttering up California commissioners because he has something to sell. He insists that "the more specific and concrete the standards are, the better the possibilities are for teachers and parents to understand what students must learn. It will also be easier for the state to assess them." Dulli's unstated assertion is, of course, that "the more specific and concrete the standards are, the better the possibilities are" for publishers to make a windfall profit. Standaristos and salesmen march to the same education drum: Teach what you can test, and we'll provide everything you need for kids to score well on those tests.

The March 12, 1998, Full Commission Meeting minutes have a quality of surreal buffoonery about them, sort of a *Who's On First?* meets Fellini. Summary is impossible. The website is http://www.ca.gov/goldstandard. Check it out. It is also illuminating to check out the state of California web page. It lists categories assumed to be of interest to browsers: History, Travel, Doing Business, Living, Working, Natural, Environmental. *Education* is not listed. Listen to them long enough, and bureaucrats reveal the truth.

AND GOD REVISED THE PLAN, SAYING, "LET THERE BE PHONEMIC AWARENESS"

First, God said, "Let there be light." Now the California State Board of Education skills posse has reminded Him, "You forgot phonemic awareness." The California State Board of Education just about has everybody whipped into shape. With the appearance of two documents, *California Language Arts Content Standards*, prepublication edition displayed by grade level December, 1997, and its fellow traveler, the *Draft Reading/Language Arts Curriculum Framework K–12*, written by Deborah C. Simmons and Edward J. Kameenui, appearing June 12, 1998. Why two documents? As explained in the introduction to the *Standards*, the *Standards* "represent a strong consensus on the skills, knowledge, and abilities all students should be able to master at specific grade levels"; the *Framework* serves as a guide "for teachers, administrators, parents, and other support personnel to know when to introduce and how to sustain the practice of skills and knowledge leading all students to mastery."

Whew! It rather takes one's breath away. Together, these documents deliver everything students and their teachers need to know. Reality check: One must realize just what "strong consensus" means. I have talked to hundreds of teachers and parents in California and not one has any idea of what is in either of these consensus documents. Consensus is when the political party in power has enough votes to ignore all dissenters. Strong consensus is when people in power are from a state adoption state and the publishers line up to publish books to align with their hobbyhorses. In this case, the co-conspirators are the Academic Standards Commission, the

Curriculum Development and Supplemental Materials Commission, and the California Board of Education.

The key words, rushing along in a torrent, make me break out in a rash:

- all students
- content to be mastered
- align the curriculum
- when to introduce
- how to sustain
- knowledge leading all students to mastery.

And we're only through paragraph two of the 75-page *Standards* document. The verbs used in the Kindergarten standards are significant: *Identify* (6 times), *know, follow, explain, recognize* (3), *distinguish* (4), *track* (3), *blend, produce, count, match, read, understand, describe, locate, use* (2), *connect, retell, ask, answer, listen* (2), *write*. This sounds like a whole lot of workbook pages to me. Where are words like *enjoy, savor, laugh, contribute, help, try out, experiment, discover*?

In 1965, scientist-philosopher David Hawkins wrote a beautiful little essay titled "Messing About in Science," an essay that circulated in the teacher underground for nine years until a collection of Hawkins' essays was published (*The Informed Vision*, Agathon/Schocken, 1974). Hawkins starts out by quoting from Kenneth Grahame's *The Wind in the Willows*.

> "Nice? It's the only thing," said the Water Rat solemnly, as he leant forward for his stroke. "Believe me, my young friend, there is nothing—absolutely nothing—half so much worth doing as simply messing about in boats. Simply messing," he went on dreamily, "messing—about—in—boats—messing—"

The concept of kids and teachers "messing about" was at the heart of Elementary Science Study, and it transformed my teacherliness more radically than any other pedagogical idea I've encountered. That's what I do: Mess about. Standardistos seem intent on cramming the day so neither teachers nor children have thirty-three seconds left over for thinking, never mind messing about. In their defense, the Standardistos did use the word "share" one time. They used it in the context of listening and speaking comprehension: "Share information and ideas, speaking audibly in coherent, complete sentences." So when kids share, they have to be sure there's a subject and verb in every utterance.

Kindergarten becomes a place obsessed by systemizing language.

- Count the number of letters in syllables and syllables in words.

- Match all consonant and short-vowel sounds to appropriate letters.

- Identify and sort common words.

And so on. Kindergartners are expected to "Locate title, table of contents, name of author, and illustrator." They are not expected to "laugh at the sound of words" or "exhibit pleasure in a story." They are expected to "distinguish fantasy from realistic text." Kindergartners. It's called "raising the bar."

Grade One Standards zero in on *systematic vocabulary development*, using the verb "identify" nine times. Other significant verbs include *blend, distinguish, respond, follow, print legibly, capitalize correctly, recognize, segment.*

- distinguish initial, medial, and final sounds in single-syllable words.

- blend two to four phonemes

- segment single syllable words into their components

And so on.

It is useful and even necessary for teachers to have both a broad outline of children's development and a set of "skills"appropriate to that development. Most excellent teachers I know keep in the back pockets of their minds a rough outline of expectation, one that leaves lots of room for individual differences, lots of room for daily surprises.

AVOIDING DOGS WHO WEAR COATS

Under *Literary Response and Analysis*, the *Standards* for students in grades one through eight state that students "read and respond to a wide variety of significant works of children's literature. They distinguish between the structural features of text and the literary terms or elements (i.e, theme, plot, setting, and characters)." Literary response thus becomes a matter of technique. Prove you are a good reader by examining structural elements: Choose the right setting in a multiple-choice question. No mention is made of asking students why they suppose the character felt/behaved the way he did, how the story made them feel, and so on. No, the Standardistos want to develop little pedants, literary technicians who can identify plot, setting, character, plot, setting, character. On and on through the grades: Plot, setting, character, plot, setting, character. It is numbing and nonsensical. If teachers follow these strictures for inspecting the techniques of stories, they will develop a nation of comatose children who hate books.

If anything, the Standards are even worse for high schoolers, further distancing them from the personal impact of literature. For grades nine and ten:

- analyze and trace an author's development of time and sequence, including the use of complex literary devices (e.g., foreshadowing, flashbacks)

- recognize and understand the significance of a wide range of literary elements and techniques, including figurative language, imagery, allegory, and symbolism, and explain their appeal

- analyze how a work of literature is related to the themes and issues of its historical period

For grades eleven and twelve:

- trace the development of American literature from the Colonial period forward

- evaluate the philosophical, political, religious, ethical, and/or social influences that shaped characters, plots, and setting

- analyze recognized works of world literature from a variety of authors, in order to

    1) contrast the major literary forms and techniques and characteristics of the major literary periods (e.g., Homeric, Greece, Medieval, Romantic, Neoclassic, Modern).[Please note the lack of parallel construction is California's style, not mine.]

    2) evaluate the philosophical, political, religious, ethical, and/or social influences that shaped characters, plots, and settings.

Who's kidding whom? And there is more. Lots, lots more. This document is seventy-five pages long. It looks more like an intellectual yard sale than a curriculum guide. Roy Blount, Jr. says studying literature at Harvard is like learning about women at the Mayo Clinic. I used to damn Standardistos for turning literature courses into a pre-Harvard pedantry. Looking at the California plan makes me see I was wrong: There is nothing "pre" about this; it's the real, miserable thing.

I would point out that it doesn't take edicts from the Standardistos to put *The Scarlet Letter* on the bestseller list. Every fall, teachers assign *The Scarlet Letter* and every fall it makes the *USA Today* Best-Selling Books list. In the fall of 1998, desperate students put Hawthorne up there with

Danielle Steel, Tom Clancy, Sidney Sheldon, V.C. Andrews, and Kathleen E. Woodwiss.

I know teachers who have done phenomenal work bringing this classic to life for teenagers. The work of Ginny McCormick's students in Allentown, Pennsylvania, for one, was published in *The New England Journal of Medicine*. That said, when we commend the classics, we have to keep our eye on the facts: Every fall, *Cliffs Notes on Hawthorne's The Scarlet Letter*, the best-selling guide for the company, outsells the real thing five to one.

The Scarlet Letter happens to be one of those golden oldies that is a great book. If teachers refused to ask the technical kinds of questions spelled out by the California Standardistos, the book might have a chance to live and breathe for students and to inform their lives. Without the technical questions, students might even forswear Cliffs Notes for the real thing.

In *How Reading Changed My Life* (Ballantine, 1998), Pulitzer Prize-winning writer Anna Quindlen talks to this point, referring to the "despotism of the educated." Quindlen observes that too many of the school discussions about books concern themselves only with the cerebral and not with the emotional. "Part of the great wonder of reading is that it has the ability to make human beings feel more connected to one another."

I wish the California Standardistos had invited Quindlen to testify. After all, E.D. Hirsch lent a hand, as did Diane Ravitch, Barbara Foorman, and representatives from AFT, from WestEd, National Geographic, Harcourt Brace, and countless other technicians who wanted to take part in setting standards. I found no evidence that the State Board of Education or the Curriculum Commissions heard testimony from anybody who spoke for a love of reading.

In recalling a childhood immersed in books, Anna Quindlen offers powerful testimony to reading for reading's sake. She notes that she didn't read because she wanted to learn something. "I read because I loved it more than any other activity on earth." This crucial point seems to elude Standardistos, who, intent on capturing the tactics of reading, seem unaware that if reading is to matter to a reader, that reader must discover that books have a soul, books can transport us. Standardistos don't quote C.S. Lewis, who observed that, whatever else we say we want out of literature, we know we "want it to take us away, away, away! into someone else's world."

Quindlen does not take on the Standardistos by name, but she does observe, "There is something in the American character that is even secretly hostile to the act of aimless reading, a certain hale and heartiness that is suspicious of reading as anything more than a tool for advancement." She refers to "careerism," an attitude that sanctions reading "only if there is some point to it." This careerism is what the California reading standards are all about. Comprehension questions on plot, setting, climax, character, and point of view. The executive set on a dogged course of self-improvement might actually learn far more from *Moby Dick* than from *The Seven Habits of Highly Successful People*. But he won't learn it from memorizing information about plot, setting, and character. The truth about reading comes from the readers, not from the standards.

Standardistos, of course, emphasize "the quality and complexity of the materials to be read by students." Anna Quindlen points to her childhood of reading indiscriminately, making no distinction between, say, *A Girl of the Limberlost* and *Pride and Prejudice*. Quindlen observes that "children who have critical judgment are as dreadful and unnatural as dogs who wear coats."

The California Language Arts Content Standards document doesn't call on experts for authority in making reading prescriptions. The document provides just three resources in the References section:

Copi, Irving M. and Carl Cohen, *Introduction to Logic*. Eighth Edition. New York: Macmillan. 1990; Harris, Theodore L. and Richard E. Hodges, ed. *The Literacy Dictionary, The Vocabulary of Reading and Writing*. Newark, Delaware: International Reading Association. 1995; *Webster's Collegiate Dictionary*, Tenth Edition. Springfield, Massachusetts: Merriam-Webster, Inc. 1996.

It is sadly apparent that the people who wrote the orders for how reading must be taught to millions of children are inspired only by definitions, never by transfigurations, never by words of testimony about the way books can thrill readers.

IN SEARCH OF JOY IN
READING/LANGUAGE ARTS STANDARDS

The Field Review DRAFT Reading/Language Arts Curriculum Framework K–12, issued June 12, 1998, by the Curriculum Frameworks and Instructional Resources Office California Department of Education, uses the words *Systematic* and *sequence* 131 times in its 230 pages of advice and admonition to teachers. The word *joy* is mentioned once, on page nine. Reminder: This is the document that "provides the instructional context for the Language Arts Content Standards approved by the California State Board of Education in November 1997." It announces "the beginning of a new era in teaching the language arts, particularly in the teaching of early reading." It calls for a balanced language arts program and then immediately defines "balance" as "the differential instructional emphasis of specific skills and strategies at strategic points in a learner's reading instruction to ensure proficiency of all language arts standards."

The *Framework* states its purpose as elaborating on the *Standards* and describing the curriculum and instruction necessary to help students achieve mastery. The *Standards* specify "what to teach"; the *Framework* specifies "how to teach it." The *Framework* acknowledges in passing that the language arts are useful for "a variety of purposes," but the aim is "to enable students to participate fully in society and the world of work." This document does list forty-seven references but ends up being self-referential, basing its support on two documents produced by the California Department of Education.

As noted above, the document does contain the word "joy." On page nine, it says, "A comprehensive program ensures that students learn to read and write, comprehend and compose, appreciate and analyze, perform and enjoy."

The California Standardistos' mission is for students to attain proficiency in the English language arts "to ensure their academic, social, personal, and economic success in today's society and tomorrow's world" and "to provide a blueprint for curriculum and instruction to make optimal all students' potential as producers and consumers of language." Consumers of language. There is the heart of the matter. Standardistos treat language like so many economic goods. The *Framework* positions itself as being useful *to a range of consumers*, including staff developers, reading specialists, library media teachers, principals, teachers, parents, publishers. Note the inclusion of publishers. The *Framework* is set up to show publishers exactly what the Standardistos want the textbooks to look like. Publishers were invited to be in on the Standards-making process from the beginning and they are the real audience. Standardistos don't care whether or not teachers read these documents. When the textbooks are on the shelves, the Standardisto mission is successful.

"Direct, explicit, and systematic instruction" isn't just for phonics. In grades four through twelve, this method of drill and practice is provided in word-attack skills, spelling and vocabulary, comprehension skills, text-handling and strategic reading skills, specific writing skills and strategies, and specific listening and speaking skills and their application.

And if by grade four, after four years of intensive direct, explicit, and systematic instruction in phonics, a student does not exhibit mastery of these prerequisite fourth-grade skills, he must loop back to direct, systematic instruction in phonemic awareness, phonics, and so on. There is no hint that if four years of this systematic "instruction" doesn't work, it might be a good idea for the skills provider to try something else. Stop the conveyor belt. I want to get off.

There are so many loony statements that it's hard to know where to begin and where to stop. I repeat just two of them, because they underlie the problem with all Standardisto proclamations.

- Academic and social expectations are well established and explicitly taught at the school and classroom levels. Classroom and school-wide discipline plans and procedures are implemented consistently by all staff.

- A commitment and plan of action is established to ensure that all students read and write at grade level.

The key words here are, of course, "explicitly" and "implemented." Standardistos believe that teachers teach and students learn. Standardistos use words like *model, pace, reinforce, question, correct,* and *feedback* to describe what Standardisto teachers must do. No teacher with more than twelve minutes of classroom experience needs proof that this is not true, but for the reader who is interested in a classroom anecdote that illustrates this point, see Chapter Seven for what happened when I set out to teach geography.

I wonder what kind of mind can write that if one has commitment and a plan of action, all students will read and write at grade level. This is totalitarian prose at its worst. Such a statement insists that all teachers from a child's earlier grades who admit that some of their students did not read on grade level lacked both commitment and action plans. I wonder what kind of mind can write this tripe. I also wonder what kind of committee-think can approve it.

SEX STANDARDS

For some years, I've been carrying around direct, explicit, even systematic (in its own loopy way), evidence that students do not learn what we teachers think we are teaching. Every time I make a keynote speech, I carry these overheads in my briefcase, thinking I just may pull them out.

But I always lose my nerve. People read my essays and assume that in public I probably stand on the podium and dance the fandango. I figured this out when I first started attending NCTE conventions. I'd get invited to parties, and before the evening was over the disappointment of the inviters who thought I'd be the life of the party was palpable. They'd say something like, "I didn't expect you to be so quiet." At parties, I'm the wallflower, the one standing in the back, not the one turning cartwheels or singing "Le Marseilles." So as a shy person, I have never used the overheads that I made from Virgil's penis papers. It's easier to put them in a book than flash them at a live audience.

Several seventh graders walked into my language arts class, griping about the results of a four-page exam on the male reproductive system they'd just gotten back in health class. Virgil, known among his peers—and his teachers—as the stud of seventh grade, had received a grade of ten percent for his knowledge of penile parts. Later, I rescued his exam from my trash can and, ever since, it's been my emblem for teaching and learning in seventh grade.

In the name of "standards," the teacher of a health course originally intended to provide immediate and practical information for twelve- to fourteen-year-olds is required to transmogrify* the course into a Standardisto pre-anatomy farce. The teacher must take a topic of intense interest and importance to pubescent kids and intellectualize it, making sex look like just one more dull school subject, with the penis just about as interesting as the apostrophe or Washington's battle plans. That's okay with Standardistos, who use their devotion to rigor as a smokescreen for avoiding the possibility of truly educating for democracy. Note that Virgil can't even locate the penis on the diagram. Can anyone in the universe believe that Virgil does not know where his penis is? Or what he can do with it?

By any traditional measures, the teacher of this course has "standards" and they are standards that fit well with the welfare overhaul bill passed by the 1997 Congress, a bill setting aside $250 million to teach children about abstinence. To qualify for the monies, localities must teach abstinence and must *not* teach birth control. In one of the videos approved for use in this program, when a student asks, "What if I want to have sex before I get married?" the instructor replies, "Well, I guess you'll just have

*In honor of the four years of teacher inservice courses I took from New York University, I try to find a place to use this word at least once in most things I write.

PART ONE : MATCHING...........MATCH THE CORRECT RESPONSE FROM
COLUMN B. WITH THE APPROPRIATE TERM IN COLUMN A.

1. Penis
2. Semen
3. Urethra
4. Testicles
5. Puberty
6. Scrotum
7. Circumcise
8. Sperm
9. Pubic Area
10. Foreskin

A. the flat tube inside the penis which carries urine or semen

B. the organ used for elimination and reproduction

C. the sac like container that holds the testis

D. the organ which stores urine

E. the area around the sex organs

F. a mixture of sperm cells and lubricating fluids

G. the age at which sex glands make reproductive cells

H. the male reproductive cell

I. a loose flap of skin that covers the tip of the penis

J. the removal of the foreskin to expose the glan penis

K. produce sperm cells

Male Reproductive System (Side View)

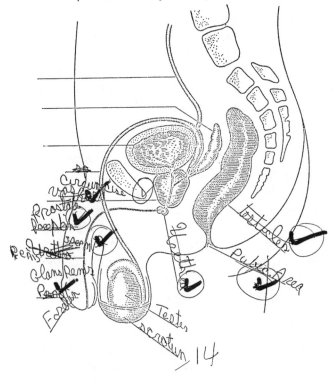

to be prepared to die. And you'll probably take with you your spouse and one or more of your children."

Be prepared to die! Now that's a slogan to which I'll march—or even dance on any podiums that come my way. But seventh graders who are convinced of their own invulnerability? Who's kidding whom?

Instead of demanding that everyone look at our schools through some rear-view mirror tinted with rose-colored glass, we should ask, Whom is school for? Whose purposes does it serve? For whose benefit do we design curriculums? Standardistos won't talk about how stultifyingly boring school is for most kids above the age of ten; standardistos are spending their time making sure school will be just as boring for kids below the age of ten.

I don't know many adults who could sit quietly through even one day of a typical dusty school curriculum. Any adults who are looking for a place where sitting and listening are required can attend a meeting of the California State Board of Education, whose meetings last five hours, "plus or minus," as they indicate in their meeting announcements posted on the web. Actually, with the Board, meeting times are kind of "buyer beware." On their web page they state: "ALL TIMES ARE APPROXIMATE AND ARE PROVIDED FOR CONVENIENCE ONLY. THE ORDER OF BUSINESS MAY BE CHANGED WITHOUT NOTICE."

In the style of a third-grade writer who wants to make sure you're paying attention, the capitalization is in the original. Actually, I love the proclamation "All times are approximate," and would certainly buy a T-shirt so inscribed. And I just might march to such a slogan. Who could predict that such a delicious directive could come from those Standardistos in Sacramento? I plan to use it immediately, such as when my husband looks for dinner precisely on the hour.

Although one may legitimately ask just what convenience is being provided with such a statement, I have to admit I'm in awe of the very cheek of this motley crew. Teachers should take note of this derring-do: Standardistos decree the time and order with which you must perform your daily rounds while announcing their determination to stick to their own approximate ways.

Actually, I don't want to find myself in close contact with the kinds of adults who would sit still for the lunacy of the Standardisto school day, particularly the middle school/junior high day. But Standardistos take junior high kids, kids whose reading ability ranges from pre-primer to twelve-plus, kids consumed by their hormonal spasms, and insist these kids sit quietly for six hours and:

- identify similes in poetry

- document reference sources with footnotes

- analyze the geographic, political, economic, religious, and social structures of civilizations of Islam in the middle ages, of China in the middle ages, of the Sub-Saharan civilizations, of Japan in the middle ages, of Europe in the middle ages, of mesoamerican and Andean civilizations

- extend the use and understanding of the inverse relationship between exponentiation and root extraction to perfect square monomials

- know the characteristics that distinguish plant cells from animal cells, including chloroplasts and cell walls

Anybody who witnessed eighth graders at a northern California school in March of 1998 taking the role of "dogs" roped up in harnessed teams and "mushers" in a one-and-a-half mile trek through hauled-in snow and other constructed hazards probably can't be blamed for fearing Standardistos may have a point. This was the second annual school Iditarod and the culminating event of a month of intensive study integrating mathematics, history, geography, art, science, and language arts. Such a project sits perilously close to self-parody, but because I had intimate contact with hordes of seventh and eighth graders for ten years, I say if you're determined to require all eighth graders to read *Call of the Wild*, maybe this is a good way to get them through it. Close encounters with seventh and eighth-graders showed me know that a curriculum that gets them moving around is to be desired. And if asked, any eighth grade teacher in the country could produce a little list of students she'd like to see trussed up in those rope harnesses.

SO WHOSE IS BIGGER?

In no way do I wish to imply that California is unique in its production of oppressive Standardisto manifestos. Standardistos in most of the fifty states are high on skills amphetamines, engaged in what amounts to a Standards arms race. In November of 1997, the New York State Regents declared that, in the name of high standards, every student would take three years of a foreign language and pass a state exam in that language in order to receive a high-school diploma. After plenty of negative publicity and public ridicule, the regents backed down. Carl T. Hayden, chancellor of the board of regents, acknowledges that people thought "we were bereft of our senses." So far, nobody in Califonia seems to be exerting much pressure on the California Standardistos to come to their senses. I have talked to hundreds of Californians who just shrug. They are convinced that this, too, will pass.

One *mea culpa* doesn't mean there still isn't plenty of nonsense to go around in New York State. For starters, there are new requirements that, to get a high school diploma, every student must pass regents exams in English, math, science, history, and social studies, exams now required only for the college-bound students who want a regents diploma, forty percent of the total of current graduates. Speculation among teachers is that the only way for this to work is to make regents exams easier, thus raising standards for the bottom and lowering them for the top. Nobody seems willing to discuss why we have to treat students like sardines, jamming everybody into the same standards tin.

These days, every Standardisto is looking for ten minutes of fame, proving "my standards are tougher than your standards." If John Silber, chairman of the Massachusetts State Board of Education, has his way, students will read from a core list, including Milton's sonnets and *Moby Dick*. Now you know and I know that anyone who says high schoolers should read *Moby Dick*:

1) doesn't know any fifteen-year-olds

2) has never read *Moby Dick*

3) has read *Moby Dick*, has a fifteen-year-old in the house, and wants to get even.

I worry that a whole lot of the Standardistos' curriculum exists on this "get even" premise. I suffered through *A Tale of Two Cities*. Why should today's kids get a break? The sad thing is that *Moby Dick* is a great book. It wasn't until I was forty-two years old that I'd sufficiently recovered from my college experience to try it again. Or, I should say, to read it for the first time. In college, I was dragged through it and passed a test on it. Okay, I confess: At forty-two, I still skipped the rope-tying stuff. It just seems a pity that in the name of Standards, we ruin so many wonderful books by forcing them prematurely on kids. For those who want to get a jump-start on standards, *Moby Dick* is available as a picture book (Farrar Straus Giroux, 1997). It will come as no surprise that the story line is so compressed that just about the only thing recognizable is the title.

I SAY IT'S THE GEOGRAPHIC, POLITICAL, ECONOMIC, RELIGIOUS, AND SOCIAL STRUCTURES OF CIVILIZATIONS, AND I SAY TO HELL WITH IT

To use a word much used in the *California Language Arts Standards*, my above remarks about seventh graders *foreshadowing* the contents of the proposed *History/Social Content Standards* were an attempt to prepare the gentle reader for what comes next. It ain't pretty. Sometime back, a number of blue-ribbon commissions expressed concern that American kids were getting too little history. Now California produces a document showing us how to give them too much.

Here's paragraph three:

> "The standards serve as the basis for statewide assessments, curriculum frameworks and instructional materials, but methods of instructional delivery remain the responsibility of local educators."

Right. As representatives of the state, the Standardistos get to decide what will be taught, the texts used to teach it, and the tests taken to make sure it was taught. "Local educators" are left to provide "instructional delivery." Thus, the avowed purpose of the Standardistos is to obliterate teaching.

More than seventy people reviewed this document: Eminent historians, geographers, economists, and political scientists, or so we are told. I suppose that's why we are told that kindergartners will describe the human and physical characteristics of places by "constructing maps and models" as well as identifying legend references on maps. First graders describe direct and representative democracy, make maps, and learn to sing "My Country 'Tis of Thee." Fans of Woodie Guthrie need not apply. And it's not hard to figure why. Kids who learn to sing the less popular verse of "This Land Is Your Land," kids singing about hungry people standing in line by the relief office, might ask unsettling questions. For teachers who want to show their students a little representative democracy in song, verse, and picture, while at the same time offering a sense of the continuity and the discontinuity, the symbols, icons, and traditions, the sense of community across time, I commend a spectacular picture book: *This Land Is Your Land*, words and music by Woodie Guthrie with folk art oil paintings by Kathy Jakobsen, and afterword tribute by Pete Seeger (Little, Brown, 1998).

First graders "know and understand the symbols, icons, and traditions the United States that provide continuity and a sense of community across time in terms of: American symbols, landmarks and essential documents such as the flag, the bald eagle, the Statue of Liberty, the U.S. Constitution, and the Declaration of Independence; explain the people and events associated with them."

The people and events associated with the Constitution? First graders? Plenty of people denounced the National History Standards for not teaching appreciation of the Constitution, so the California Standardistos make sure California kids will have the Constitution coming out of the kazoo.

Just when you think it might be safe to go out at night, here comes 1.6 of the California History/Social Science Standards:

"Students understand basic economic concepts and the role of individual choice in a free-market economy, in terms of:

1. The concept of exchange and the use of money to purchase goods and services.

2. The specialized work that people do to manufacture, transport, and market goods and services and the contribution of those who work in the home.

Remember, this is Grade One.

Second graders label a map of North America from memory: Countries, oceans, Great Lakes, major rivers, mountain ranges. Second graders also read the biographies and "explain how heroes from long ago and the recent past make a difference in others' lives. The Standardistos suggest: George Washington Carver, Marie Curie, Louis Pasteur, Albert Einstein, Indira Gandhi, Abraham Lincoln, Jackie Robinson. I sense E.D. Hirsch's influence here. The peculiarity of the grouping as well as its developmental inappropriateness has that Hirschian feel to it.

Third graders do pretty much of the same plus they learn the three branches of government and also learn:

3.4 How California, the other states, and sovereign tribes combine to make the nation and participate in the federal system.

3.5 Students demonstrate basic economic reasoning skills and an understanding of the economy of the local region, in terms of:

1. how local producers have used natural resources, human resources and capital resources to produce goods and services in the past and the present

2. how some things are made locally, some elsewhere in the U.S., and some abroad

3. how individual economic choices involve tradeoffs and the evaluation of benefits and costs

Fourth graders get latitude and longitude and the Spanish missions. Many California teachers won't see much new here. I remember studying the Spanish missions in fourth grade eons ago. Of course, the text then, like the text today, does not talk about Father Serra's missions as a system of forced labor. And in my youth, latitude-and-longitude (linked together as the school's reanimation of a geographical Bobbsey twins) didn't cast its awful pall until fifth grade. With *Longitude: The True Story of a Lone Genius Who Solved the Greatest Scientific Problem of His Time* (Walker, 1995), Dava Sobel actually put longitude on the best-seller list. This surely suggests that nothing is "wrong" with longitude, anyway. What's wrong is when Standardistos try to shove it into children's consciousness at a developmentally inappropriate age. Kids memorize it as "Some lines go one way and some go the other." Kids perceive it as the schools present it: A technical problem. Sobel made the best seller list by showing all us former fifth graders that the study of longitude is the study of human drama, ingenuity, and persistence at its best.

In the new California standards, fifth graders "describe the entrepreneurial characteristics" of early explorers such as Columbus and Coronado. They also "understand the purpose of the state constitution, its key principles, and its relationship to the U.S. Constitution (with an emphasis on California's Constitution.)" Actually, I, a native Californian, have vague memories of learning—no, memorizing—all that California Constitution stuff. I wonder today, how much poorer a life I lead for not remembering a bit of it for longer than six minutes after regurgitating the facts on a test. All I remember is the bear on the flag.

There is more matter here than I can possibly describe. This document reads like the outline for at least half a dozen fat college texts. One thing that catches my eye is that fifth graders are expected to understand the course and consequence of the American Revolution, in terms of, "5.5 identifying and mapping the major military battles, campaigns and turning points of the Revolutionary War, the roles of American and British leaders, and the Indian leader alliances on both sides."

This, for me is deja voodoo. I started my teaching career watching my seventh grade remedial readers refuse to draw those battle plan maps, and after thinking about it for five minutes, I refused to urge them to reconsider.

A lot more is expected of California fifth graders: The shortcomings of the Articles of Confederation; the principles of the Constitution; the defining role of economic incentives and the effects of the physical and political geography and transportation systems in terms of the waves of immigrants from Europe between 1789 and 1850. It will come as a relief to parents that Standardistos want fifth graders to learn the old chestnut "the location of the 50 states and the names of their capitals." That is definitely something the kids can do. Whether there is any point to it is another question. Seeing something kids can do comes as such a relief that I don't even care whether they *should* do it.

Sixth, seventh, and eighth graders:

- distinguish relevant from irrelevant information, essential from incidental information, and verifiable from unverifiable information in historical narratives and stories.

- assess the credibility of primary and secondary sources and draw sound conclusions from them.

- students detect the different historical points of view on historical events. . . .

I wonder why the media mavens reporting on the Standards fail to distinguish relevant from irrelevant information, essential from incidental information, verifiable from unverifiable information in the documents. I wonder why the media fail to assess the credibility of primary and secondary sources and draw sound conclusions from them.

Standard 7.9 is the penultimate standard. Seventh graders, who as you may recall from above, already had to learn the history of civilization in medieval times, now under 7.9 will analyze the historical developments of the Reformation, in terms of:

1. the causes for the internal decay of the Catholic church (e.g., tax policies, selling of indulgences)

2. the theological, political, and economic ideas of the major figures during the Reformation (e.g., Erasmus, Martin Luther, John Calvin, William Tindale)

3. the influence of new practices of church self-government among Protestants on the development of democratic practices and ideas of federalism

4. the location and identification of European regions that remained Catholic and those that became Protestant and how the division affected the distribution of religions in the New World

5. how the Counter-Reformation revitalized the Catholic Church and the forces that propelled the movement (e.g., St. Ignatius of Loyola and the Jesuits, the Council of Trent)

6. the institution and impact of missionaries on Christianity and the diffusion of Christianity from Europe to other parts of the world in the and early modern periods, including their location on a world map

7. the "Golden Age" of cooperation between Jews and Muslims in Medieval Spain which promoted creativity in art, literature and science, including how it was terminated by the religious persecution of individuals and groups (e.g., the Spanish Inquisition and the expulsion of Jews and Muslims from Spain in 1492).

Seventh graders meet John Calvin! William Tindale! The Council of Trent! The prospect leaves me breathless. Surely a person must be unusually dense to think seventh graders can be forced to drink of this brew. I confess I thought it wonderfully apt that William Tindale is of such secondary significance that he isn't even in my *Merriam Webster's Collegiate Dictionary: Tenth Edition*. But I kept checking and discovered that he's there. Standardistos, ever esoteric, employ the third-alternate spelling.

SEEKING ASYLUM FOR SEVENTH GRADERS

Time out. Does anybody out there know any seventh graders? As a refresher course, let's hear from premier New Hampshire middle school teacher Linda Rief. This description of emerging adolescence as both the best of times and the worst of times is from her book, *Seeking Diversity: Language Arts with Adolescents* (Heinemann, 1992):

> Working with teenagers is not easy. It takes patience, humor, and love. Yes, love of kids who burp and fart their way through eighth grade. Who tell you "Life sucks!" and everything they do is "Boring!" Who literally roll to the floor in hysterical laughter when you separate the prefix and the suffix from the word "prediction" and ask them for the root and what it means. Who wear short, skin-tight skirts and leg-laced sandals, but carry teddy

bears in their arms. Who use a paper clip to tattoo Jim Morrison's picture on their arm during quiet study, while defending the merits of Tigger's personality in *Winnie-the-Pooh*. Who send obscene notes that would make a football player blush, written in pink marker, blasting each other for stealing or not stealing a boyfriend, and sign the note "Love, ____ P.S. Please write back."

Nancy Doda of National-Louis University in Virginia, speaking for "thinking about who seventh graders are," read this passage from the podium at the National Academy of Sciences, to a convocation of 450 experts who had gathered in September 1998 to discuss how best to teach mathematics to these seventh graders. Some math professors in the audience looked as though they had been pole-axed.

No one who knows seventh graders would insist that the subject matter will take precedence for longer than about twelve minutes a period; that's on good days. "Bad-mannered little shits" is a phrase that seventh-grade teachers understand. It was coined by Noel Coward, referring, not to seventh graders, but to the Beatles.

And the above is just one of eleven standards that California Standardistos say seventh graders will master in their history classes. Seventh graders face similarly impossible lists for five or six other classes. If I were a parent in California, I would be looking for a job transfer out-of-state rather than face the savage reality of the homework these standards will generate. A class-action lawsuit against the Board of Education might be another possibility.

I have not checked with Jon Scieszka about whether his little fable in *Squids Will Be Squids* (Viking, 1998), is an anti-paean to California's history standards, but it could be. Titled "Grasshopper Logic," it centers on a homework assignment:

"Rewrite twelve Greek myths as Broadway musical. Write music for Songs. Design and build all sets. Sew original costumes for each production."

California eighth graders seem to have an easier time. They analyze the political philosophy underpinning the U.S. Constitution as specified in "The Federalist Papers," the significance of Jefferson's State for Religious Freedom, the principles of federalism, and so on. Lest anyone think that Mark Twain's remarks buried James Fenimore Cooper's awful prose forever, Cooper has been resurrected by these California Standardistos, who advise eighth graders to read him to learn about the daily lives of people in early national America.

In grades ten through twelve, students do all sorts of neat things, including conducting benefit/cost analyses and applying basic economic indicators to analyze the aggregate economic behavior of the U.S. economy. Students are commended to read biographies of John Locke and Jean-Jacques Rousseau, among others. I wonder if they'll read about Rousseau abandoning his five illegitimate children at the front door of the local orphanage. I can't imagine what they will read about Locke. Tenth graders get both the first and second World Wars and the rise of totalitarian governments. Eleventh and twelfth graders actually have much narrower focuses than any previous grades except kindergarten. Eleventh graders get "turning points in American history in the Twentieth Century"; twelfth graders "pursue a deeper understanding of the institutions of American government." They also "master fundamental economic concepts, applying the tools (graphs, statistics, equations) from other subject areas to the understanding of operations and institutions of economic systems. All those teachers who struggled with statistics in graduate school will be happy to learn that twelfth graders master it.

An interesting footnote: No history/social studies standards have been written for ninth graders in California "in deference to current California practice in which grade nine is the year students traditionally choose a history/social studies elective." I have read all the standards documents, including the minutes of commission meetings, produced by the California Standardistos. In twelve grades of imperatives and explications, this is the only mention of students getting a choice.

The people writing these history standards are trying hard not to offer explicit direct instruction but to get the students to dig deeply and to analyze. So why am I whining? These fellows paid too much attention to verbs and gave no consideration at all to developmental appropriateness, that's why. Anyone who thinks that seventh graders are going to analyze "St. Thomas Aquinas' synthesis of classical philosophy with Christian theology" isn't just whistling in the wind; he's out to lunch.

California Standardistos were very conscious that these are the first-ever statewide academic standards for history, very conscious of what happened to the National History Standards, a document that ninety-nine senators voted to condemn. The hundredth senator later said he'd misunderstood the question and had also favored condemnation. A lot of people criticized these national standards because they did things like omit mention of Ulysses S. Grant while mentioning Harriet Tubman six times. Maybe that's why the California standards have included everything but the proverbial kitchen sink. Some people think the ugly denunciation of these national standards pretty much squashed the impetus for a string of national documents. Ramsay Seldon, of the Council of Chief State School Officers, says "There's absolutely no interest now in having any kind of national activity on standards. The whole issue has become like a political toxic-waste dump, and nobody wants to go near it." For a fascinating account of the whole affair, see "Playing Games with History," by Karen Diegmueller and Debra Viadero, *Education Week*, November 15, 1995.

In announcing the California Academic Commission's approval of its standards, History/Social Science Committee Chair Lawrence Siskind said, "Our History/Social Science Standards are balanced and academically rigorous. I am especially proud of the civic values and virtues which they impart. When they graduate high school, California students will be ready to vote, to serve on juries, and to take their place in society as responsible citizens. Should they ever be called upon to fight for their country, these standards will teach them why their country is worth fighting for."

No comment.

AND THE VERB STANDS ALONE

On April 1, 1998, at a Full Commission Meeting, someone noted that action had been taken about the verbs in the history document. Quoting directly from the minutes, "CLEANED UP THE VERBS . . . LOOK AT VERBS." And from kindergarten on, the people writing the History/Social Science Standards have made an obvious and serious attempt to avoid verbs frequently used in the Language Arts documents, verbs like *match, distinguish, recognize, track, identify, connect, use, follow, blend, segment, know, apply, locate, discern, show.* Here are the verbs from the Kindergarten History Standards: *demonstrate, match, compare and contrast, determine, distinguish, construct, demonstrate, understand.* Here are verbs from the Seventh Grade History Standards: study, *examine, analyze* (used ten times), *compare, and contrast.*

Verbs also ended up being crucial in the mathematics standards document. The Commission on Academic Performance and Content Standards sent in the math standards they'd approved. Then the Board of Education made substantive changes, including a heavy edit of the verbs. State Superintendent of Public Instruction Delaine Eastin asked the Board not to do it. She said, "They've deleted verbs like model, understand, estimate, interpret, classify, explain, and create, and the verb they most commonly substituted was compute. Essentially, this comes down to the fact that we are going to teach kids to add, subtract, multiply, and divide, and we're not even going to let them use a calculator before the sixth grade."

Here's an example that shows how important verbs can be: The standards commission's initial proposal said that second graders should be able to "create and solve" simple problems. The State Board revised this to read pupils should "solve" the problems. "Instead of getting a child to have to think by creating a problem, they just want to get the answer," said Sonia Hernandez, a top Department of Education official who represented Eastin on the standards commission.

The standards commission spent a year writing the guidelines for math instruction. According to Board of Education member Marion Joseph, the resulting document still lacked "clear, complete, and correct" statements about what children should know. Joseph is one commissioner who insisted on her right to serve on both the language arts and the mathematics panels. Part of the "correction" by the board includes state tests that require seventh graders to find square roots without calculators. Joseph insists that letting kids use calculators makes the problem-solving more like "math appreciation" than real math. She says the State Board of Education believes the way "to get children to do more and better and higher math" is to say to teachers and students, "do it, solve it, know it."

Joseph's pronouncements confirm one more time that Standardistos don't know what they are talking about. Read the memoirs or biographies of great mathematicians and scientists and you will find a common thread: Real math is an appreciation for the beauty and pattern of our number system; it is this appreciation that draws young children into a rigorous study of mathematics. Nobel prize physicist Richard Feynmann wrote passionately on this topic; he also wrote passionately about the lunacy of trying to serve as a consultant to the California State Board of Education.

BANNED IN CALIFORNIA

My biases are already pretty apparent. I'm definitely not a Platonist and reject the Standardistos' attempt to make the inscription on his door universal: *Let no one enter who does not know mathematics.* I'd rather see schools teaching kids how to read food labels than order them to study the *Chicago Manual of Style.* One of my favorite poem titles is Gary Snyder's "Removing the Plate of the Pump on the Hydraulic System of the Backhoe." I wonder what Standardistos would make of this, busy as they are insisting that teaching poetry consists of making sure kids can identify simile and metaphor.

I must make a statement of truth in disclosure. I am one of the people who applied to the California State Department of Education to become an inservice provider. When, on December 22, 1997, I applied to become a professional development provider in California, I found out about Section 24.03 of the 1997–98 Budget Act, prohibiting the use of Goals 2000 funds for any program that encourages inventive spelling techniques in the teaching of writing. Harkening back to the loyalty oaths of post-McCarthyism, I had to sign an "assurance clause," indicating that I would comply with the invented spelling prohibition. It has always seemed ironic to me that people devoted to phonics wouldn't celebrate the phonics-derived invented spelling techniques young children use because they are anxious to try out hard words in their writing, but that's another story.

I had it on good authority that no rogue reading teachers need apply. But I like a challenge, and so I spent two days filling out the application. I confess I was driven as much by curiosity as by challenge. Actually, I followed the letter of the law. I proposed to teach phoneme awareness through rhyming picture books and word games; to teach systematic explicit phonics skills through tongue twisters and poetry; comprehension through multiple versions of the same fairy tales and riddle writing. And so on. Following the guidelines provided by the California Department of Education, I also submitted copies of any handouts I might want to give to teachers and any overhead transparencies I might want to show them. The California Department of Education stipulated that my syllabus must include thirteen specified components. They also specified the percent of time I should spend on certain components.

The funny thing is that everybody I know who applied—people of diverse pedagogy—Connie Weaver, Brenda Power, Patrick Shannon, Shelley Harwayne, Bobbi Fisher, Jim and Kathleen Strickland, Margaret Moustafa— all received the same boilerplate rejection letter. We come from all around the country. I had not talked with any of them about applying, but I am proud to be in such good company. I later saw half of a dozen of the applications and can testify that the content of our applications couldn't have been more different, reflecting our very different approaches to literacy learning. What's more, people in this group of rejectees are in much demand, giving keynote speeches and workshops at literacy conferences around the country and in foreign countries. We were judged by the California Department of Education to be identical in our deficiencies: We did not meet *Criterion #4*, which, as far as I can figure, means our handouts and overhead transparencies weren't in the right order.

Criterion 4. The syllabus shall indicate the order in which printed materials, as well as audio, video, and other technology-based resources, are planned for distribution or use and demonstrate how each of these materials or resources relates to the component(s) being addressed. All written materials intended for distribution, as well as audio, video, or other technology based resources, intended for use, during the proposed professional development which are provided for review shall be, as closely as possible, consistent in quality and content with those actually to be distributed and used.

CDE staff may determine that either a) the materials or resources are sufficient in quality, content, and order, or b) the materials or resources, in whole or in part, are insufficient in quality, content, or order to support the proposed instruction; are internally inconsistent; or are inconsistent with the instruction envisioned by Chapter 3.45 or 3.46 or Part 25 of the Education Code, as applicable, and other provisions of the California Reading Initiative and, on that basis recommend the application for disapproval.

Whew! Thanks for sharing.

The folks disbursing these Goal 2000 funds promised to let each unsuccessful applicant know just where she erred. The regulations of the California Education Code state that if an application is disapproved, "Applicants shall have the right to modify their applications during the review process in order to meet the evaluation criteria." Once rejected, I wrote, asking for help in revising my application to meet the criteria. I tried phoning, but the voice mail at the Professional Development Unit was always "full," indicating, I suppose, that a lot of people received Criterion 4 rejection letters.

My plea to these people for help eventually elicited another form letter, this one from the Chief Deputy Superintendent, Educational Policy, Curriculum, and Department Management, written on the letterhead of Delaine Eastin, State Superintendent of Public Instruction. Since in my letter I had said I needed help interpreting Criterion 4, the repetition of Criterion 4 in their reply seemed rather like, when trying to give directions to someone who does not speak your language, you just keep repeating the words louder and louder. The Sacramento people added one final paragraph, informing me that the application submission period for fiscal year 1997–98 is over and thus my application cannot be revised to meet Criterion 4.

In one of those serendipitous moments, Yetta Goodman happened to be standing in line to get a book signed by an adolescent book author at the International Reading Conference in San Diego. People started talking about the California standards and Yetta mentioned that she did not apply to offer professional development because she knew she was "banned in California."

A California teacher standing next to Yetta was incredulous. "What do you mean? How could you be banned?" Yetta said it was common knowledge that the Goodmans' names should not even appear in applicants' bibliographies. The California teacher said, "I don't believe it!"

Someone else in line resonded, "Oh, yes. It's true. I had my proposal accepted, but I had to redo it first."

Yetta asked, "Did you have to go to Marion Joseph's garage to be reviewed for final approval?"

"No, I wasn't in her garage. It was the main part of the house. There were four of us there waiting for our turn for advice on our proposals. When it was my turn, Marion Joseph went through my proposal page by page. She said a section on invented spelling had to be removed. Then she found a page with a quote by Patricia Cunningham that talked about reading in context; she said that had to be removed. Then she found a quote by Ken Goodman; she said that had to be removed. Finally, she asked me to remove certain citations from my bibliography."

Yetta asked this "accepted in California" staff developer if she would write up this amazing tale. The woman apologized, noting that she works full time as a staff developer and cannot afford to jeopardize her livelihood. Besides, she said, if this is the way California education officials want it, it must be okay.

What bothers me about all this is not that phonics phreaks won out over whole language zealots. In the past, I have complained publicly when some misguided whole-language adherents attempted to assert their devotion to "good literature" by denying Random House, the publisher of a series of junky Ninja Turtle books, display space in the exhibition hall. Never mind that Random House also published quite wonderful books; I defend the right of Ninja Turtles to have their place on the table. When anybody in power decides to make choices for teachers, this results in the deskilling of teachers, the insistence that teachers need guardians and gatekeepers, and are incapable of making their own curriculum decisions. When any committee sets itself up as judge and jury of what words of advice teachers should hear, weak teachers are hurt because their opportunities to grow are limited; strong teachers are hurt even more because an administrative lust for conformity will end up driving them from the profession. The students are hurt most of all.

Bill Honig didn't trust teachers when he was superintendent of schools in California and pushing literature lists, not phonemes. Then, to get state funds for trade books, teachers had to choose books from pre-approved lists and *Tale of Two Cities* continued to be a classroom staple. Now that Honig, a free-wheeling education entrepreneur, has found phonics, and is director of the Center for Systemic School Reform—and a successful applicant to be a provider of inservice training in California schools—he still insists on deskilling teachers by not allowing them to make curriculum choices. Honig announces that "education must become more like medicine, must become much more diagnostic." Then he sets himself up as both chief diagnostician and the drug seller.

Why aren't teachers protesting? Why aren't they storming the citadel of the California Department of Education and the state legislature? California teachers take the same attitude as teachers everywhere: If you don't like the way the people in charge are doing things, just wait a couple of years and they'll decide to do it differently. Certainly this is true in California as perhaps in no other state.

A basic principle that Standardistos don't grasp is that a skill in context in a classroom or in real life is worth fifty bushels of "gold standards" filed away in state board of education vaults. Of course, teachers are hoping that's exactly where they will be filed. I have asked 108 California teachers the same question: What do you think of the standards? Not one has seen them. Their attitude is the attitude of teachers nationwide: *This, too, will pass.*

READING THE SMALL PRINT

I had just completed the computer spellcheck on this chapter when the mail came. Because of my "exclusive age and occupation group," I received an offer for burial benefits. After being immersed for six weeks in the California standards, I rather feel like I could use such benefits. The tone of the language in this burial document is similar to the tone of the Standardistos—confident and, believe it or not, upbeat, making lots of promises: Do this and you'll get this. There is such an air of buoyancy that I almost forget I have to be dead to collect. The part I like best about this burial benefits policy is that it offers *guaranteed satisfaction.* Pardon me? Of course, when you read the small print, it means I'll be satisfied with the policy they send me; there is no guarantee about how I'll feel towards the resulting interment.

Junk bond salesmen are similarly clever at inventing deceptive names for risky bonds. Customers don't buy junk bonds; they buy "high yield" bonds. Frank Partnoy, author of *F.I.A.S.C.O.* (Norton, 1997), says the best piece of advice he ever received was from a manager who suggested he could become an expert in emerging markets simply by telling people he was an expert in emerging markets. That's what he did, confessing to the reader that his expertise in the Japanese economy is based on Speed Racer cartoons and Godzilla movies.

Likewise, the Standardistos' assumed expertise in subject matter arises from very dubious premises. I can't fathom on what they base their notion of child development. But they take their cue from junk-bond sellers: You become an expert in matters of the schoolhouse by declaring yourself an expert in matters of the schoolhouse. And it doesn't hurt to have some governors and the President and the CEO of IBM grinning at your side.

Standardistos are intent on training students that school is work, separate from the frivolity of leisure. I believe in bringing tons of frivolity to the work. That's why no third grader ever got out of my class without standing at my side and reading riddles, and why seventh graders had to listen to me read *Flat Stanley* aloud. In an interview about his writing, Max Apple was asked, "How do you keep a balance between your serious intentions and your sense of play?" Apple replied, "Playing is the most serious thing I do: Always." I would say the same about reading riddles in third grade. It was the most serious enterprise I undertook with those children.

Reading the pronouncements of the California Standardistos brings us back to Dr. Spock, who offered parents some advice that teachers should heed: *You know more than you think.* These standards documents attempt to strip teachers of their knowledge, their intuition, their pragmatic savviness, their flexibility, their very hearts. I hope California teachers will pass through their classroom doors every day chanting, "You know more than *they* think, you know more than *they* think." I know that teachers are tougher than they think they are. What worries me is the kids. I don't know if they are tough enough to survive these standards.

One California teacher who despairs told me, "Why don't they just build the jails next to the schools?" Interesting idea. Since 1980, California colleges and universities have downsized 8,000 jobs. The state's prisons have upsized by 112,000 inmates and 26,000 guards.

The California Standardistos walked down the wrong path from the start. Their statutory requirements were to produce standards that:

- must be measurable and objective

- must reflect the knowledge skills necessary for California's work force to be competitive in the global, information-based economy of the 21st century.

Not surprisingly, Standardistos do not invoke the name of John Dewey. As Nel Noddings has observed, possibly Dewey's greatest insight was to build educational strategy on the purposes of the child. "This does not imply letting the child learn what he pleases; it suggests that, inescapably, the child will learn what he pleases." The teachers' job, then, is to prepare an environment that will stimulate and challenge children to want to learn worthwhile things.

In *The Ecology of Fear* (Henry Holt, 1998), Mike Davis points out that Southern California's multibillion-dollar flood-control system was built to control a statistical abstraction called the "hundred-year flood," which, in fact, has already occurred twice in this century. Likewise, California's curriculum control system has been built to control a statistical abstraction called the student: a student who is not likely to occur in any century.

6

It's The Economy, Stupid

PIZZA HUT, MERIT PAY, AND OTHER FLIMFLAM

*M*ale baboons exchange greetings by yanking on each other's penis. I don't know how Fortune 500 CEOs, media pundits, and politicians greet each other, but I do know that only one percent of their DNA differs from that of baboons and that ninety-nine percent of what they say about public education is hooey. And worse. And if one hundred baboons sat in a computer lab, they'd produce *Moby Dick* sooner than one hundred CEOs would tell the truth about the relationship of their advocacy of one-size-fits-all educational standards to upsizing/outsizing their own salary packages, the sideswiping of middle- and working-class America, and the subsidy of state-of-the-scam sports stadiums with their corporate luxury suites, and the push for tax-supported vouchers to private education.

In the spring of 1990, a special "Saving Our Schools" issue of *Fortune* magazine kicked off the decade-long corporate escalation of school-bashing. "Why are American kids worldclass dunces?" asks a staff reporter, and then launches the knee-jerk litany we can all recite automatically: Kids in Japan do more homework, kids in Japan clean the school toilets, kids in

Japan. . . . *Fortune* points to one bright spot on the U.S. educational horizon, lauding the *Pizza Hut Book It!* reading incentive program for "creating a real appetite for learning" (pun presumably intended). I have denounced this bribery boondoggle before, and I acknowledge that plenty of teachers who have to rent public storage space for their stockpiles of gold stars and "Good Work!" stickers disagree with me. But whether they agree or not, teachers understand that when students do work for the sake of a reward there is a different feel to the process from when children are engaged in an activity for its own sake. I understand the ever-present lure to grab hold of some short-term benefits, but teachers need to consider that a program that hands out pizzas to kids for saying they read a book may be producing fat kids who don't like to read.

The education reporter for *The New York Times* cannot fathom what I'm talking about. After I denounced *Pizza Hut Book It!* in a *Phi Delta Kappan* deconstruction of the tenure of Secretary of Education William Bennett, who praised the program, *The New York Times* reporter phoned me, asking, "What's wrong with pizza?" I tried to explain the harmful effects of external reward systems in the classroom—and in society at large. I tried to explain that I worked hard at helping my students come to the love of reading for reading's sake, not for the sake of a six-inch-diameter pizza or some other geegaw. I explained that in my classroom when a child finishes reading a book, his reward is getting to read another book. I tried to explain that if we hope to *educate* our children, to help them develop good character traits, help them develop autonomy, persistence, and judgment, then we must help them savor learning for its own sake, not because somebody is keeping a scorecard and handing out trophies. I told him it doesn't matter whether those trophies are gold stars or pizzas, they seriously diminish children's growth toward autonomy.

There was a long silence on the other end of that phone line. The reporter was baffled; he was even speechless. And when he did get his voice back, he just kept asking, "What's wrong with pizza?" "Don't kids love pizza?" The trouble is, of course, that education reporters feel a lot more allegiance toward corporate America than toward the schoolhouse. I knew it was futile, but nonetheless I launched into my spiel that Pizza Hut could demonstrate its support of reading by donating books to school libraries, and those libraries could hang brass plaques to acknowledge this generosity. I said maybe Pizza Hut had figured out that when they gave an eight-year-old a six-inch-pizza, the family that drove her to the restaurant to pick up her prize would probably spend fifty bucks on their pizzas and sodas. The

New York Times reporter just figured I'm an ungrateful nuisance. After all, schoolteachers are supposed to be grateful for corporate handouts—even when they undermine education. *The New York Times* should change its motto from *All the news that's fit to print* to *All the news we can understand*.

Funny thing, W. Edwards Deming's warnings about merit pay are pretty much in line with my concern about pizza bribes. Deming's personal story is the stuff of legend. Revered by Japanese business, he was, until fairly recently, unknown in his own land. By now, corporate America has embraced Deming, at least on paper. But a tenet of Deming's business philosophy that gets little publicity, in the U.S., anyway, is his advocacy of the elimination of pay-for-performance. Deming argues that people are not motivated by money (here the *New York Times* and *Fortune* and the U.S. Department of Education could substitute the word "pizza"); what motivates them is self-esteem and the love of learning. In an interview in, are you ready for this? *Forbes* magazine (May 27, 1991), Deming debunks the idea of merit pay. Deming says that ranking people results in demoralization, and that when employees are scrambling to achieve better personal ratings, these narrow, short-term goals sabotage the company for which they work. W. Edwards Deming says, "This country was built on cooperation," and for that reason he advocates, after taking seniority into account, paying every employee in the same job roughly the same wage. He advocates uniform raises, not raises based on merit. Deming says such a system builds teamwork, and teamwork builds a better company than competition.

All this sounds strikingly like the system by which teachers are paid in most states, the very system so under attack by corporate mavens, the U.S. Department of Education, newspaper editorialists, and others who insist that the merit of teachers can and should be rated like slabs of beef, and that they should be paid accordingly. Deming disagrees. "Performance cannot be measured. Merit pay is not merit pay. Differences may be caused by the system. It's rewarding the circumstances. Same thing as rewarding the weatherman for a pleasant day." Now when you think of raising the standard of teacher performance by giving them merit pay, just consider all the destitute weathermen during the Gulf Coast hurricane season or New England ice storms.

EDUCATION SUMMITEERS

On March 27, 1996, President Clinton addressed those gathered at the National Education Summit at Palisades, New York. And quite a gathering it was. The Planning Committee included the governors of Wisconsin, Nevada, Colorado, Iowa, Michigan, and North Carolina, as well as business leaders from IBM, AT&T, Bell South, Eastman Kodak, Procter & Gamble, and Boeing. Participants included governors and business executives from forty-three states. Geography standardistos as well as conspiracy theorists can figure out which states aren't represented—and why. Extra credit if, like fifth graders across the land, you can name all the capitals: Alaska, Arkansas, California, Colorado, Connecticut, Delaware, Florida, Georgia, Idaho, Illinois, Indiana, Iowa, Kansas, Kentucky, Maine, Maryland, Massachusetts, Michigan, Mississippi, Missouri, Nebraska, Nevada, New Hampshire, New Jersey, New Mexico, New York, North Carolina, North Dakota, Ohio, Oklahoma, Oregon, Pennsylvania, Rhode Island, South Carolina, South Dakota, Texas, Utah, Vermont, Virginia, Washington, West Virginia, Wisconsin, and Wyoming.

The list of people invited as "resources" is fascinating. Here are a few of my favorites:

- Lynn Cheney, American Interprise Institute

- Denis Doyle, Heritage Foundation

- Chester Finn, Hudson Institute

- Diane Ravitch, New York University

- Secretary Richard Riley, Secretary of Education

- Albert Shanker, American Federation of Teachers

- Lewis Solmon, Milken Foundation

- Bob Schwartz, The Pew Charitable Trusts

So you didn't get invited if you weren't a proven lapdog of the Corporate/Conservative Think-Tank Standardistos. Special consideration seems to have been given to those who write op-ed pieces for the *Wall Street Journal* praising vouchers and denouncing public education. And, of course, The Pew Charitable Trusts, charitable to *Education Week's* hatchet job on the schools titled *Quality Counts* (see Chapter Seven), not so charitable to the diversity of public education. But as Rush Limbaugh told his radio audience on June 5, 1998, "Diversity has nothing to do with the greatness of America." For Standardistos, diverse standards are an oxymoron. For me, standard standards are both a insult and an impossibility.

When IBM hosts an education conference on Standards, they invite resource people who demand that teachers don the pin-striped, avaracious attitude of a Michael Milken or an Ivan Boesky, not that of a Ralph Nader or a Mother Jones. The junk-bonds-dealer-mentality is welcomed; social activists and bleeding hearts need not apply. But who needs respect when they've got liquidity?

When he addressed the group, President Clinton said, "I accept your premise." Clinton's education agenda had been apparent since his Arkansas days. Hillary Rodham helped negotiate Bush's America 2000, the precursor to Goals 2000. And it gets worse. Clinton continued: "I accept your premise; we can only do better with tougher standards and better assessment, and you should set the standards. I believe that is absolutely right. And that will be the lasting legacy of this conference. I also believe, along with Mr. Gerstner and the others who are here, that it's very important not only for businesses to speak out for reform, but for business leaders to be knowledgeable enough to know what reform to speak out for, and what to emphasize, and how to hammer home the case for higher standards, as well as how to help local school districts change some of the things that they are now doing so that they have a reasonable chance at meeting these standards." President Clinton used the word *standards* forty times in his short speech. President Clinton talked about a "full-meaning" high school diploma; about "meaningful standards" that would "require a test for children to move . . . from elementary to middle school or from middle school to high school." He said that in our global society, a "full-meaning" high school diploma ought to mean pretty much the same thing in Pasadena, California, as it does in Palisades, New York.

I think of Keith, who, by anybody's test, would never make it out of primary school. I wonder if the Summiteers will build new schools to house these seventeen-year-old second graders. In the face of ninety percent of the children I taught, the words of these Summiteers are either carelessly half-baked or deliberately mendacious. People whose computers have whistles and bells can *hear* the President's words on the Internet at www.summit96.ibm.com

Denis Doyle, who bills himself as "education analyst," and who co-authored *Reinventing Education* (Dutton, 1994) with Louis Gerstner, as well as *Winning the Brain Race: A Bold Plan to Make Our Schools Competitive* with David Kearns, was present at this education summit. Doyle denounces anybody who tries to point out factual errors in popular attacks on public education. He says *The Manufactured Crisis: Myths, Fraud, and the Attack on*

America's Public Schools (Addison-Wesley, 1995) by David Berliner and Bruce Biddle is "anti-intellectual" and filled with "errant nonsense" in its assertions that Chester Finn, Bill Bennett, and Diane Ravitch, among others, work against public education. Doyle then refers to the great *Education Week* Standardisto Ron Wolk, publisher of *Quality Counts*, (discussed in Chapter Seven), as a "dispassionate observer." Wolk had presented a typical Standardisto response to *The Manufactured Crisis*, labeling as "absurd" the authors' charge that the "crisis" in public schools is the product of deliberate corporate disinformation; Wolk damned the book both as paranoia-based and crassly commercial. I think by "commercial" Wolk might mean that the book, unlike so many education tomes, is actually readable. And Berliner and Biddle ask the pointed question that nobody in the media seems to be asking: Why would corporate CEOs argue that American schools do not produce enough workers with technical skills when the personnel directors of those businesses insist it's the habits of mind, not the math skills, that most concern employers? Doyle decries this interpretation as evil. Now look up on the participants' list for this education summit, taking note of participant Doyle's affiliation, and then tell me I'm paranoid because I see a conspiracy against public education.

There have since been two more books that support the case made by Berliner and Biddle: *The Truth About America's Schools: The Bracey Reports 1991-97* (Phi Delta Kappa, 1997), by Gerald Bracey and *Shell Game: Corporate America's Agenda for Schools* (Phi Delta Kappa, 1997), by Clinton Boutwell. Bracey's work is a collection of his data-based analyses of the condition of public education that appear each October in *Phi Delta Kappan*. Bracey's findings, in sharp contrast to the prevailing corporate/political/media view, are must reading. He's no Pollyanna, but he does give us hope. Overall, he finds that schools are about as effective as they have ever been, though they serve a population dramatically harder to educate. Bracey's conclusions in his first report matched those of a group of systems engineers at Sandia National Laboratories in Albuquerque whose report stating those positive conclusions was suppressed by "internal politics." This is not to say that Bracey doesn't see a need for schools to change. In his words, "One need not assume school failure to propose school reform."

A portion of Boutwell's book also appeared in *Phi Delta Kappan*. Its premise, documented with lots of facts and figures, is that, contrary to the claims of big business, U.S. schools and colleges are producing lots of well-qualified graduates, but there aren't enough high-paying jobs to go around. Boutwell says that business executives like Gerstner want educators to produce more and more students with high-tech skills, building a large labor pool from which he and his cronies can choose "the pick of the litter" and pay them low wages. And before you can say "competition is what makes America great," workers need a B.A. plus the ability to lift fifty pounds to work in a warehouse.

All this just goes to prove that when politicians and corporate leaders sit down at an education summit table, count the forks. Noted educator Seymour Sarason says that to call the inexcusably ahistorical, acultural report emanating from this summit "superficial" is to be too charitable. But the governors heeded President Clinton's message when they got back to their state capitals: They hammered home the business agendas. Maybe these folks are well-meaning and neither malicious nor deliberately deceptive. But when Lou Gerstner, the $91.5-million-a-year man trumpets that "standards are the sine qua non of school reform" I lock up the silver and start looking over my shoulder.

Whether the other summit attendees are well-meaning or not, one thing is for sure: They are wrong. They are wrong because they base all their recommendations on the premise that the productivity they measure in industry has a direct analog to measuring children's learning. Standardistos don't like to hear this, but we can't measure what children need to know in "productivity" units. The truth is, we can't measure them in any units that will satisfy the Standardistos.

When public figures screeching for national education standards aren't employing fatuous platitudes, they're spewing forth cooked data. This is why you should read Bracey in *Phi Delta Kappan*; he checks out the data that everybody else parrots. In the October 1998 *Phi Delta Kappan*, for example, he gives President Clinton and Vice-President Gore the "Statistics from Thin Air Award" for writing a letter to *USA Today* claiming that by 2000, "60 percent of all jobs will require advanced technological skills." Bracey provides a funny account of trying to get a citation for that chimerical 60 percent figure out of the White House, the Secretary of Education, or the Secretary of Labor.

The fiery rhetoric filling corporate boardrooms and newspaper editorials just goes to prove that where there's smoke, there's smoke. Nonetheless, teachers can't ignore the smoke. As British astronomer and physicist Fred Hoyle once observed, "Words are like harpoons. Once they go in, they are very hard to pull out." Once media headlines announce 5,683 times that public education in America is in the sewer, it's hard for mere teachers to prove otherwise. I, for one, am grateful that Gerald Bracey is there, trying to do battle against the harpooners.

I notice that former New York State governor Mario Cuomo was not invited to the National Education Summit. Cuomo, of course, is no longer governor but, more important, he asks the forbidden question: Where's the money? In the summer of 1998, speaking on WAMC, the Albany, New York public radio station, the ex-governor observed that "standards have become a cheap way for politicians to look like they're 'for' something. They don't want to pay for genuine standards. They want to give tax cuts to people who already have plenty of money."

Also notably absent from this summit meeting were teachers. Teachers, of course, have good reason to know that CEOs, politicians, think tank scholars, and media pundits may not be the best people to decide what needs to go on in classrooms across America, particularly when they're enshrining testing and social Darwinism.

FOLLOW THE MONEY

Take Louis V. Gerstner. In 1993, he went from being CEO of RJR Nabisco to being CEO of IBM, receiving a signing bonus of $4,924,596 plus a generous stock package (which *Business Week* listed at more than $21 million); in 1994, his book *Reinventing Education* (Dutton) was published, and we learned that Gerstner holds teachers responsible for not producing an increasing supply of world-class workers, which he claims IBM needs. Whenever I hear about "world-class workers," I try to follow the money. Soon after receiving his signing bonus, Gerstner fired 90,000 of IBM's 270,000 employees, the same kind of highly-trained workers he insists the schools aren't producing. But his stockholders love him. During his five-year tenure, IBM's market capitalization is up almost $70 billion. So what's a few thousand high-tech workers here or there?

Gerstner claims that one of the things wrong with the schools is the lack of merit pay. I love it when a guy making over $20 million advocates merit pay, the assumption, being, of course, that he's worth every penny he gets, but maybe the teacher making $35,000 isn't worth that much. "The best teachers and the worst teachers are paid the same," intones Gerstner. "Those in scarce disciplines are paid what those in abundant supply are paid." Under this supply and demand theory, of course, English teachers would get low pay and math teachers high. Gerstner continues, "Paying the marginally fit, or worse yet, the unfit, the same as the best and brightest invites cynicism." I'd like to tell Mr. Gerstner what invites cynicism: Having a $21-million-a-year man talk to me about *merit pay* for teachers.

Gerstner is a guy with plenty of advice for teachers. Positioning himself as an education reformer, he insists that the "business" of schools is "the distribution of information." Now there is a definition to inspire us all to work harder. And conspiracy theorists who are nervous about the Standardisto familiarity of the phrase "the distribution of information" can take another look at Chapter Five and then download the complete text of the California standards.

In *Reinventing Education,* Gerstner preaches to teachers, "Know what your job is; know what your outcomes should be; know how you will measure output." Measuring output, now there's a notion on which to build a teaching career. Maybe it's my background as a third-grade teacher, but I've never been able to embrace "output." You mop up a lot of ouput in third grade. Boston detective Spenser warns his school psychologist lady friend against using jargon. "That kind of talk will rot your teeth." When CEOs start writing books about improving the schools, take a look at their employee outputs. And then force every CEO who intones about the problems of U.S. education to examine the inputs to schools. In 1995, the General Accouting Office (GAO) reported that one-third of the nation's schools need extensive repair or replacement. Fourteen million children attend these crumbling schools. For starters, maybe we could take over the skyboxes of the major sports arenas, luxury skyboxes built by the taxpayer.

IT'S GOOFY, AND IT'S POLITICS AS USUAL

In the closing moments before the 1998 elections, the traditional time to stuff the budget with favorite pork barrel items, Congress refused to vote funds to repair our crumbling school infrastructure, but they did vote to make the world safe for Disney, granting the giant corporation an extra twenty years of exclusive rights to Mickey Mouse, Donald Duck, Pluto, Goofy, and friends. If the Disney copyright had been treated like other copyrighted material, it would have expired in 2003.

Disney chair Michael Eisner handed out PAC money to thirteen key lawmakers before the vote was taken. Speaking from personal experience, I know that Disney is not generous in granting people permission to quote from its copyrighted materials. When I asked for permission to quote from their version of "Cinderella" for a book on fairy tales to be used in classrooms, they denied permssion. Librarians fought the copyright extension, but librarians can't hand out PAC money to thirteen key lawmakers.

NOT AS SIMPLE AS ROCKET SCIENCE

Not all corporate leaders are out there waving fingers of blame at teachers. When Arco President Robert Wycoff went into the Manual Arts High School in South Central Los Angeles and took on the job of principal for the day, he saw strengths as well as weaknesses in the school. Although *Fortune* editors who interviewed Wycoff about his experience characterized it as "odd" that Wycoff should end his day "more hopeful" about U.S. education than when he started the day, Wycoff seemed to have gained real insight from talking with students and teachers. He liked the students; he respected the teachers and the principal. And he concluded, "If I were principal of Manual Arts, I could not do as good a job as I saw today." Wycoff added a very significant observation, "This is not as simple as going to the moon."

It is no wonder that the *Fortune* reporter was confused. Imagine a captain of industry insisting that running a school is a complex undertaking. Wycoff seemed to be rejecting the corporate role either as alms-giver or truth-teller, popular stances of many of his colleagues. Wycoff acknowledged that, in addition to money, technology, and advice, what is needed to revitalize our schools is ongoing conversations with the people in those schools. When those conversations occur, people on the "outside" are forced to acknowledge the strengths as well as the needs of the schoolhouse.

U.S. corporations have long been involved in education, but most of their money has gone to colleges and universities. In 1988, of the $2.1 billion donated by American corporations to educational causes, just ten percent went to public schools. There's no small irony here. Universities have received most of the money, and when something extraordinary happens, such as putting a man on the moon, the universities reap all the credit. We hear where the astronauts went to college. When do we hear about their third-grade teachers? Historically, public schools get none of the money and yet they get all of the blame for everything from teenage pregnancies to the balance of trade. One small example: Harvard invites Ivan Boesky to be a commencement speaker and declare that "greed is good," while at the same moment public school teachers are excoriated because newspaper reporters perceive they don't teach values to young thugs pillaging the neighborhood.

CORPORATE MALFEASANCE, EQUITY, JUSTICE, AND WELFARE MAMAS

National standards and measures are not devised for the elite schools in the nation. Those schools have been using different yardsticks for decades:

Gifted programs, honors and advanced placement classes. There is no better predictor of success in school than the level of schooling attained by one's parents. And the best predictor of wealth is several previous generations of wealth in the family. So the standards circling the land are based on inheritance and, in the end, these standards will be used to blame the victim. Standardistos will proclaim, "We gave them equal educational opportunities. It isn't our fault if they didn't pass calculus."

When you start thinking about education, before long you'll end up thinking not only about corporate malfeasance, but about equity, and about justice, and yes, even about welfare mamas. We live in a complex, fractured society in which the rich get richer and the poor get blamed. The number of millionaires in this country is increasing at amazing rates; so is the number of the truly destitute. One in five children who come to our schools lives in poverty. As teachers, we can't look the other way. The first step we can take is to stop blaming the victim. The legacy of *A Nation at Risk*, which appeared in 1983, is that people believe rotten schools have produced a rotten workforce and hence failure in international competitiveness. The truth of the matter is, of course, that the President and Congress and the Federal Reserve Board make policy with regard to international competitiveness. But what fun can headline writers and radio talk shows have with denouncing the Federal Reserve Board? It's a lot more fun to run banner headlines calling teachers in Massachusetts or Mississippi stupid.

When we talk about standards, we need to recognize the real issues. In the end, the standards are not about curriculum; the standards are about social justice. We have to be ever wary that the "full-meaning" high school diploma doesn't become an elitist diploma that excludes lower-class kids. As Alfie Kohn points out in "Only for *My* Kid: How Privileged Parents Undermine School Reform" (*Phi Delta Kappan*, April 1988), there is no national organization called Rich Parents Against School Reform, but across the country highly educated white parents fight to preserve a tracking system. Jeannie Oakes, author of *Keeping Track* (Yale University Press, 1996), calls them "Volvo vigilantes." Kohn wryly observes that many of them drive Jeeps.

In addition to finger-pointing at teachers, President Clinton's Goals 2000, a rehash of President Bush's education plan, is pretty much mirrors and smoke screens, offering some bread crumbs and circuses while the infrastructure continues to crumble. The claim is that improved educational standards will lead the United States to a high-skill, high-wage economy. Tell that to the twelve percent of new doctorates in physics who received no job offers. Tell that to the Domino's pizza-delivery drivers in the Washington,

D.C., area who have B.A. degrees. In *Bright College Years* (Simon and Schuster, 1997), Anne Matthews reports that one-third of the drivers have such qualifications. She also reports on a warehouse supervisor job ad for the Gap: "Bachelor's degree required, and the ability to lift fifty pounds." Politicians are selling snake oil when they insist that if teachers just pull up their socks and get standards, General Motors will sell more cars than Toyota, and all the people formerly employed in the aerospace industry will find jobs. Corporate thugs have given us a job market where Manpower Inc., the nation-wide temporary employment agency, has surpassed General Motors as the number–one employer.

As Clinton Boutwell points out in *Shell Game: Corporate America's Agenda for Schools*, not only are U.S. public schools doing their job better than ever, they are producing many more skilled students than corporate America has room for. Boutwell cites a recent Census Bureau study to the effect that "the proportion of college graduates entering the better-paid occupations—executive, managerial, and professional specialties—*declined* from 53.6 percent in 1989 to 48.4 percent in 1991."

At the same time American corporations are "outsizing," sending jobs to foreign climes with low wages, they are demanding that the schools save American business from the threat of foreign economies. Nobody is stepping up to promise that life will be fair, but corporate life is rather mind-boggling in its greed. In 1996, AT&T Chairman Robert E. Allen saw his compensation, with stock options, triple to $20 million—just as he ordered the layoff of 40,000 employees. Albert Dunlap laid off twenty percent of Scott Paper's workers, then made $100 million for himself by selling the downsized company to Kimberly-Clark. Word isn't yet in on the personal gain for Xerox top management as their reward for slashing 9,000 jobs, but Jack L. Kelly of Goldman, Sachs says, "There's a real paradigm shift here, from an engineering-driven company to one that really knows how to rip out infrastructure to get costs down."

Congressional committees spend untold millions investigating why seven people at the White House travel office lost their jobs. We can wonder when they are going to investigate why corporate America has laid off thirty million people.

Downsizing is profitable for stockholders as well as CEOs. In 1995, average executive compensation jumped twenty-three percent to $4.37 million, and at the same time 3.26 million American workers were fired. Disney CEO Michael Eisner insists that "Money is not a driving force." Speaking on National Public Radio on September 28, 1998, Eisner insisted, "I don't think about it." Eisner, one of the highest paid executives in the nation, collected $565 million in one day of December 1997—the biggest executive payday ever—when he cashed in seventy-three million shares of his Disney stock. The Disney Company provides another example of quite amazing financial chicanery. When Michael Ovitz was ousted from the presidential job at Disney because his job performance was found to be inadequate, Disney paid him at least $70 million as a "get lost" bonus. (Some estimate this figure at closer to $100 million.)

Let's assume that Ovitz put in forty-hour work weeks during his sixty-week tenure, the conservative estimate of $70 million means he got a bonus of $29,166.67 an hour for his unsatisfactory work. The last I heard of Ovitz he had joined the advisory board of the Children's Scholarship Fund, a voucher system headed by venture capitalist Theodore Forstmann and John Walton, one of the Wal-Mart heirs. Their plan is to create competition in education, "ending the public school monopoly," by giving children "matching" scholarships to parochial schools. Carole Shields, president of People for the American Way, says that the real agenda of this foundation is to push for taxpayer-paid vouchers to fund private and parochial schools. Speaking at the National Press Club on September 28, 1998, Forstmann unleashed a vicious attack on public education. The moderator noted that Forstmann had brought along his own front-row rooting section. Every ugly remark he uttered provoked laughter and vigorous applause.

In 1995, a third of all children in the U.S. lived in homes with incomes of less than $25,000, less than one hour of Michael Ovitz's bonus pay for unsatisfactory work. One in five children was in a home with an income below $15,000. When we're talking about what standards are required for children growing up in America, shouldn't we consider household income?

If the American-schools-produce-bad-workers theory were true, why did the defect rate on American automobiles fall by seventy-five percent in the decade between 1981 and 1991? Was it because third-grade teachers reformed their wicked, nonstandard ways, or maybe because someone or something revolutionized Detroit? When U.S. fourteen-year-olds finish fourteenth or eighth or whatever in an international mathematics competition (Read Bracey for how that data was cooked), newspaper headlines and television soundbites holler and harangue. Where is the thunderous denunciation of the American Medical Association because the U.S. ranks twenty-eighth in the incidence of low-birthweight infants? Japanese children outscore Americans on math tests? They also have half the risk of infant mortality.

Rather than repeating the litanies of Standardisto mumbo jumbo because of small differences between U.S. and foreign students on one test or another, our politicians and corporate moguls would do better to concern themselves with the enormous gaps in the achievement-test scores between the rich and poor right here at home. Yammering about standards, of course, has a political purpose: It shifts responsibility and perpetrates a fraud. Instead of looking at issues of poverty, teen pregnancy, drug use, violence, and the safeguarding of children, our leaders say, "Let's prove we have standards by giving a national test."

Clinton and his crew have promised that by 2000, "all students should be mentally and physically ready to learn." Then they show just how cheap political talk really is by slashing Food Stamps and abandoning the welfare safety net. Instead of fixing something as basic as the roofs and toilets in crumbling urban schools, Washington offers a few "competitive grants" to prod the states to come up with tests that measure a rise in "standards." And they give Disney extended exclusive rights to Goofy.

In 1994, the price tag to carry out repair orders in the New York City schools was $600 million. We're not talking beautification or modernization or wiring for the Internet: We're talking fixing holes in roofs, exposed wiring, nonfunctioning plumbing. The cost of instituting some sort of preventive maintenance in these New York City schools was posited at $1.5 billion. In that same year, 1994, in the name of standards, the House approved a $420 million bill. This wasn't enough to fix the toilets in New York City schools or to buy textbooks in Alabama, so the bill offered Cracker Jack prizes to states willing to mandate more tests. And these are just the schools children attend. What about the substandard housing? What about the homeless children with no homes at all? Do the politicians have a plan for making sure they are mentally and physically ready to learn?

In case you forgot what they were, here are the tenets of Goals 2000:

- All students will start school ready to learn.

- High school graduation rates will be at least 90 percent.

- Students will be competent in English, history, geography, foreign languages and the arts.

- U.S. students will be No. 1 in the world in math and science.

- All adults will be literate and skilled.

- Every school will be free of drugs and violence.

Amen.

I tried to reach the website titled *Teachers and GOALS 2000,* which "describes how teachers can use the unusual opportunity presented by Goals 2000 to step forward and lead the journey toward *high standards for all students in their schools and communities.*" Alas, I received the message "connection is unreachable," which has a fittingly otherworldly sound to it. The latest notices are 1995 progress reports on Goals 2000, which seems to suggest that the program has run out of steam in Washington. By 1998, the President was limiting his reform message to speaking out against guns in school and speaking for uniforms.

But the damage has been done. Since he made testing a national priority through his Goals 2000 bribes, state boards of education are determined to write tests, administer tests, and interpret tests. In a commentary on WBEZ radio in Chicago, reprinted in Harpers in July 1998, sixth grade teacher Daniel Ferri concludes, "At best, the tests are a waste of money. . . . Yet somewhere along the way, we stopped thinking of test scores as a tool and started thinking of them as a goal. In Illinois, so much rides on these scores—from local property values to the long-term funding schools receive from the state—that teachers are encouraged to teach the tests rather than the knowledge and skills the tests are supposed to measure."

The testing mania infects all districts, rich and poor. In his book *In the Name of Excellence* (Oxford University Press, 1991), Thomas Toch describes the loony levels to which some superintendents push their obsessions about test results. Where student art once hung in conference rooms, superintendents now hang charts of the CAT scores for every school in the district. In some districts, for two months before the CAT testing, students receive an extra hour of computer time each day to practice answering multiple-choice questions.

CRYING FOR CHICAGO

Back in 1993, when 411,000 children in Chicago couldn't start school on time because the school district didn't have enough money to open the schoolhouse doors (for the fifth time in ten years), I wrote a combination tough-minded, bleeding-heart op-ed piece for *USA Today.* I said we all must weep for Chicago, and then we must get mad as hell and do something about it. I suggested that we reassert our belief in the Fourteenth Amendment of the U.S. Constitution, our belief that we are our brother's keeper, that everyone must have equal protection under the law. We must be outraged by the devastating inequities between suburban and inner-city schools; we must abolish the repressive property tax as the means of funding schools, substituting an income tax instead. Whether we live in Vermont or Beverly Hills, when Chicago bleeds, the rest of us must bleed, too.

Predictably, that op-ed piece generated some flak. I agreed to go on a talk radio show in Arizona and also in Alabama. Each time, the host read my tax proposal on the air and then the phones lit up. Irate callers figured I must be from Chicago. Who else could possibly care about schoolchildren there? Once I'd established my Vermont credentials, the Arizonans insisted, "Well, if the people in Chicago don't like the schools, they should move." That was also the Alabama solution. If people in the Bronx, Newark, Philadelphia, Los Angeles, Fort Worth, Albuquerque don't like their schools, then they should just move. People can just pick up Jay Mathews' *Class Struggle* and choose one of the districts listed as housing America's top high schools (this list is compiled by dividing the number of advanced placement tests a school gave in 1996 by the number of graduating seniors). That's the educational plan of talk show radio: Chicagoans who are upset that their school district is broke should pick up and move to Scarsdale, Scottsdale, Bloomfield Hills, Princeton.

When I asked the irate callers what happened to the moral imperative of "Am I my brother's keeper?" they said I was preaching some sort of "left-wing religion." Similarly, as Vermont struggled to equalize its school tax structure, making sure every child gets the same support, novelist John Irving called it a Marxist plan, unfair to the wealthy.

I don't now nor have I ever lived in Chicago. Or Detroit. Or East St. Louis. Or Conecuh County, Alabama. But I have done research in their schools, and I know firsthand about the devastating poverty there. When schoolchildren anywhere bleed, so must the rest of us. If we deny having a stake in the education of all the children in this country, we deny hope for our future. Bring on the gated communities, the private security guards, the moats.

Nationwide, we spend about $5,000 to send a child to public school. We spend about $22,000 to keep a person in prison. Each new juvenile correction facility costs around $102,000 per bed to build. The average after-school program costs about $3,000 per child. In a nation that finds its national pride in being the best and the most generous, one in three children in our nation's capital lives in poverty, one in four children in New York. The figure is 30.6 percent in New Mexico, 25.4 percent in Oklahoma, 28.0 percent in Arizona. Psychometricians tell us that the correlation between lower test scores and the percentage of children living in poverty is .99.

In his call for higher standards, California's governor Pete Wilson defined the new three R's of a world-class education system as "results, responsibility, and return on investment." If that is true, then it is the responsibility of the citizenry to see that all U.S. children have an equal opportunity for an education that might help them climb out of poverty. And for starters, we need to spend the same amount of money on their schooling. In California, officialdom might start assuming resposibility for helping children become better readers by putting librarians back into the schools.

The Arizona phone-ins went ballistic at the suggestion that a portion of their taxes might subsidize schoolchildren in Chicago or Conecuh County. What they failed to realize is that we already subsidize, through federal deductions on local property taxes, national inequalities in school funding. Residents of my tiny town of Charlotte, Vermont, and residents of Phoenix, Arizona, are subsidizing the district in Texas that spends $19,000 per student while at the same time denying help to the Texas district that can come up with just $2,000 per student.

Conservative commentator George Will goes on television making pronouncements about the need for "market forces at work in schools." This, of course, is the theme song of people who advocate vouchers, people who feel that competition from private schools will force public schools to get standards, to mend their lax, lazy, and spendthrift ways. I wonder how many Fortune 500 businesses resort to bake sales to finance basic operations. How many General Motors executives collect soup can labels or cash register receipts to get the equipment they need?

When market forces are at work, Chemical Bank and Chase Manhattan Bank merge, reducing their combined workforce by sixteen percent. That's 12,000 people. News of the layoffs sent the stock value up eleven percent. So each fired worker increased the stock value by about $216,000. A *New York Times* writer suggested that if the bank had fired all the employees, they could have increased their share value by another fifty-three percent. In 1799, Thomas Jefferson observed, "Banking establishments are more dangerous than standing armies," but the attitude of most of corporate America scares me as much as banks do. They all seem intent on the quick buck, with no thought of building for the future.

The Arizona callers were candid about pinning their hopes on California's Proposition 174. Getting defeated doesn't stop the voucherists. They have plenty of support to try again. Proposition 174 would have provided public tax dollars to any group serving twenty-five children to start its own religious school. Witches, vegetarians, Hare Krishnas, flat-Earthers,

Rosicrucians, vivisectionists, Elks, and John Irving—they all get their own school. Well, to be fair, Irving has started his without vouchers. But from what I can tell, the moral imperative of people objecting to an equal education for all is the following: Lock the door, load the gun, and pray for vouchers.

NOBODY PROMISED YOU A ROSE GARDEN—OR A HIGH TECH JOB

Standardistos make promises for the future. Once teachers start teaching with standards and students wake up to the fact that they have to attain these standards, then when, say, ninety percent of the kids in Harlem successfully complete algebra, foreign language, and all the other bells and whistles attached to the new high school diploma, all those Harlem kids will find some patron to send them to college and they'll major in computer science or electrical engineering—and when they get out of college they'll get good jobs at IBM, right? Like Ronald Reagan said, "We live in the future." Right.

It turns out that not only is there nobody promising rose gardens, nobody's really promising high-tech jobs, either. According to *The Wall Street Journal* and a whole lot of other institutions that look at these sorts of things, the five million workers needed between 1996 and 2006 include engineers, health care workers, special education teachers, social workers, musicians, and designers. There will be plenty of demand for service occupations: Home health care aides, child care workers, and manicurists. *The Wall Street Journal* does not reveal the very low salaries paid to these workers in the service occupations. Reporters just get very caught up in the fact that there are a lot of manicurists in this country. Why would a kid be inspired to keep high standards in her studies for, at best, $16,000 a year?

At the same time the Clinton administration advocates standards in the name of a national test, Congress and the President erase our nation's responsibility to its poorest citizens. The arrogance of the people in power was brought home to me on May 19, 1998, when the Senate rejected a proposal to limit lawyers' fees in tobacco cases to $250 an hour. I was particularly interested in this vote by Senators, most of whom are lawyers, as I had just returned from Washington D.C., where I read proposals for the National Science Foundation. Officials there told us that Congress had set our remuneration at $260 a day plus a plane ticket. From that, we had to pay our expenses. So if we chose a hotel carefully and walked the twenty-three blocks to NSF headquarters, we could break even. Maybe. Four months later, I haven't received my $260. Government functionaries ask educators to donate their time for the good of standards. I was pleased to be asked do it but I do wonder if the lawyers think $250 an hour is enough pay for their own coffee. The NSF provided coffee and cookies for us proposal evaluators, and they collected $2.00 from each of us to pay for these snacks.

A SEVEN-YEAR HIGH SCHOOL PLAN

I grew up listening to stories about the fact that it took my dad seven years to get through high school. He would go to school a year and then drop out a year and work at menial jobs to help support his family. Hey, I wasn't sure anybody who shot thirty-six rattlesnakes before breakfast needed a diploma, but Dad seemed to take more pride in his skills as a grave digger. He was such a good grave digger that he was offered a supervisory job at the cemetery, a chance to wear a suit. But he figured he'd better go back home and finish high school. My mother's mother was the first single parent I knew. She trekked from Oklahoma to California with three children—sleeping under the car at night. I heard stories about that journey from my grandmother. My mother would never talk about it—except to forbid me to read *Grapes of Wrath*. I've always wondered how people with those experiences could be Republicans, but these days even Democrats are Republicans, and we can't count on anybody's political party for much. These days, politicians of every stripe develop their own cottage industries centered on fixing family values while taking away food stamps, though of late tough talk of sending the children of the poor to orphanages seems to have lost cachet.

Years of teaching have shown me that distressed family circumstances can destroy children, but I also know that important family values are passed on no matter what the family circumstances. If you read the right books instead of trying to cook the books, you can get that same message. Standardistos would do well to read about how important government support, i.e., welfare, has been to children of single-parent, welfare mamas who grew up to go to Yale and Brown.

In *Unafraid of the Dark* (Random House, 1998), Rosemary Bray, a former editor of *The New York Times Book Review*, describes growing up poor in Chicago in the 1960s and becoming one of the first black women at Yale. She tells how her mother's decision to apply for welfare saved the family, allowing Rosemary and her siblings to get an education. She concludes that none of this would have been possible if her mother had been forced into a low-wage job and thus not been home to protect her children. Rosemary

Bray observes that she is "living proof of the seventy-eight percent of African-American women who are raised on welfare but never return to the system. (For whites, the figure is only slightly lower—76 percent.)"

The other twenty-two percent are usually teenagers who become pregnant before finishing high school. One can wonder why welfare reformers, and those concerned about what our schools offer students, don't get together and do something for these pregnant teenagers, something other than removing the welfare safety net for families.

In *A Hope in the Unseen* (Broadway, 1998), Ron Suskind tells the story of Cedric Jennings, the son of a jailed drug dealer and a high-school dropout who decided when he was two years old to quit her job as a secretary and go on welfare. In reordering her priorities, she decided, "A child either gets the love he needs or he doesn't." Cedric's mama planned quite deliberately how to give him a loving, sheltered life in the midst of the cocaine-dealing, crime-infested Washington D.C., neighborhood in which they lived. Cedric's mamma bought him used books; she took him to the museum and she took him to the library. They spent a lot of time at church. When he started school, she went back to work.

Anyone who cares about school, about standards, about social justice, and even about dorm life in the Ivy League in the nineties won't be able to put this book down. You'll laugh and you'll cry, and you'll know why you are a teacher. This vivid chronicle of three in years in the life of a boy's academic life has sex, drugs, rock and roll, mathematics, and a whole lot more.

Cedric refuses to appear at an academic awards ceremony at his high school because awardees are jeered at and attacked by their fellow students. In their way, his social battles at Brown are even fiercer. Of course the intellectual challenges are excruciating. I defy anyone to read about Cedric's second midterm exam in calculus and keep a dry eye. Or read how he and his roommate tormented each other without laughing out loud. As a sidenote: In these present times when it is so popular to decry the tumultuous sixties and early seventies as causing all our present troubles, the quite touching as well as pragmatic behavior of one of Cedric's classmates, the son of those sixties radicals Bill Ayers and Bernadine Dohrn, certainly makes their parenting skills look good. I found myself saying, "Well, all right!" to this kid. Any parent would be proud. As the teacher who remains grateful for the teaching philosophy she found during those years, I say, "Thank you!"

Standardistos should know that I found Cedric's first visit to the Brown bookstore heartbreaking. This straight-A high-school student sees all these books and he is frightened, realizing that these books are foreign to him but familiar to other Brown students. He picks up a thick biography of Winston Churchill, thinking, "I probably should know who this is." And so, as I read this, I give a brief, very brief, nod to E.D. Hirsch. First the nod and then the frozen, silent contemplation of the reality of a kid like Cedric. I can't read on, but sit contemplating all the things this boy doesn't know.

Even without Churchill, Cedric moves ahead. And the reader comes away from this book knowing that education standards are not in the numbers but in the kids. What we need to examine are not the printouts of SAT scores but the lives of the children. Standards don't mean a thing without a mama like Cedric's.

In the end, Cedric's ignorance of the identity of Winston Churchill isn't an argument for E.D. Hirsch's *Cultural Literacy*. In the end, Cedric's story is an argument for keeping mothers and children on welfare, an argument for the power of the dream, the power of hard work, the power of pride (and mixing in just enough religious humility so that your pride doesn't get you killed).

Without pride and arrogance, this kid would have been obliterated—if not by the slums, then by the rich kids at Brown. Or wiped out by calculus. Mostly, of course, Cedric's story is an argument for having a tough, loving mamma who goes on welfare until her child starts school—to give her baby a loving start in life—and then who fights for that boy. And never misses PTA. In one of the most touching scenes in the book, even after Cedric has his acceptance letter from Brown (and has made twenty copies to show people), his mama puts on her good clothes to attend PTA. She has "been going to PTA meetings for a dozen years. Never missed one, even during the worst times, and she isn't about to miss one now."

Read this book in tears and in laughter. Read it to break your heart. Read it to give you hope. Read it for the standards offered by a mama, not those spewed forth from a committee of Standardistos. Read this book knowing that Cedric's mama probably could not achieve her feat today. As our politicians and corporate moguls work to standardize schools, they have put the welfare system into chaotic freefall. For the first time in sixty years, there is no federal guarantee of assistance to poor women and children. States can do as they wish, and thus we see a "race to the bottom" of public assistance for poor children at the same time we are demanding that schools train these same children to score at the top of "world class standards." When the governor of Mississippi, for example, can say that the only assistance he plans to provide for poor women is an alarm clock so they can get to their workfare jobs, we should look carefully at the standards that are operating.

To support the Personal Responsibility and Work Opportunity Reconciliation Act of 1996, men stood in the halls of Congress, calling welfare mothers like Cedric's and Rosemary's alligators and leeches.

If we're going to call welfare mothers alligators and leeches, what do we call Bill Gates for spending fifty million bucks on his house? Lucky? What do we call the unnamed couple who opened up the Missyplicity Web site to explain why they gave $2.3 million to Texas A&M to try to clone their twelve-year-old border-collie-and-husky-mix pet dog? For a timeline on this project as well as anecdotes about Missy written by her "human mother," who prefers this term to "owner," just tune in at www.missyplicity.com. Viewers of this site learn that this project is not a joke: "Cloning a dog is largely a matter of the right talent—which we've assembled—combined with sufficient time and money—both of which we have."

There you have it: When you have money, you can do what you damn well please, be it building an ostentatious house or giving your dog a page on the Web. Or having the media take you seriously when you tell teachers how to do their jobs.

Nobody gets rich worrying about the children. At a minimum, the Personal Responsibility and Work Opportunity Reconciliation Act of 1996 puts 1.2 million children into poverty. Where's the responsibility and opportunity in that? You cannot treat human beings as animals and then expect them to achieve world-class standards. At the very time we hear daily stories illustrating that excess has become a way of life for the very rich, we cut off minimal safety nets for children. The 1996 Congress that insisted on giving the Pentagon $9 billion more than it requested, at the same time cut $54 billion from child nutrition programs.

In 1960, corporate CEOs earned forty-one times what their workers made. In 1995, they made 185 times the amount. One hundred and eighty-five and climbing fast. Fortune 500 CEOs averaged $7.8 million each. This is more than the average salaries of 226 school teachers. *Vanity Fair* puts Bill (as in billion) Gates' 1998 worth at $60 billion. The magazine suggested that with his fortune he could buy 46 air-force stealth bombers or 6,000 army Blackhawk helicopters. Or he could buy four years at a public university for every eighteen-year-old in the U.S. Or he could have Habitat for Humanity build a three-bedroom house for every homeless person in the country. Or he could buy every sports team in major-league baseball, the N.B.A., N.F.L., and N.H.L.—and still have thirty billion bucks left over.

According to *The State of America's Children*, the 1998 yearbook of the Children's Defense Fund, since 1989 the poorest fifth of the families among us have lost $587 each; the richest five percent has gained $29,533 each. "We have five times more billionaires but four million more poor children." Sixty-nine percent of the 14.5 million poor children in this country live with parents who go to work every day. Their parents work, but they do not make a living wage. This, not the math scores on international tests, is the shame of America.

If we want to talk about standards in the schoolhouse, we must talk about standards in things like the minimum wage. We must talk about giving every child a fair start in life before we worry about whether or not he's going to take algebra or score higher than the Japanese on a test. While we wring our hands about international standards in children's mathematics scores, we should consider the fact that the poverty rate among U.S. children is higher than that of any other advanced industrial nation. Depending on what test you look at and when you look at it, we rank fourth or tenth among industrialized countries in math scores. We rank seventeenth in rates of low-birthweight babies. Funny how we don't hear much about that. One wonders if a $8.7 trillion economy, an economy that spends $30 million every hour on armaments, cannot afford minimum standards of care for its children. It was that raving liberal former five-star general, President Dwight Eisenhower, who said in 1953 that armament spending "Is not spending money alone. It is spending the sweat of its laborers, the genius of its scientists, and the hopes of its children."

In 1995 and 1996, a Republican Congress raised the proposed level of defense spending by $20 billion more than the Pentagon asked for. Although the U.S. spends more on defense than all its declared or potential adversaries combined, in 1998, President Clinton joined the Republicans, inviting the Pentagon to ask for more money. And when you pay $2 billion per bomber, $3 billion per submarine, and $5 billion per aircraft carrier, it adds up. In 1998, the tab for books for all the K-12 school libraries in the U.S. was $451.6 million.

The 1996 welfare law quite literally took food from the mouths of children, slashing food assistance programs. Over $20 billion from the food stamp program over six years. That's about one month's worth of national defense spending. We can predict what these food cuts will do to the scholastic achievement of poor children. The Children's Defense Fund reports a sixteen percent jump in requests for emergency food aid in twenty-nine cities nationwide. One in five of these requests went unmet simply because the food pantries ran out.

Deny children the basics in their homes and how can we continue to up the ante on what they will be able to learn in school? In the last century Alexis de Tocqueville observed "America is great because America is good, and if America ever ceases to be good, America will cease to be great." But we can go back farther than that for a guide. "You shall not pervert the justice due to your poor." Exodus 23:6. More of the left-wing religion.

According to the U.S. Department of Education, about thirty-three percent of low-income youth are in college in October following their high school graduation. More than eighty percent of high-income youth are in college. In 1979, the maximum federal Pell grant to low-income students covered 77 percent of the cost of attending a public college; in 1993, it covered 35 percent.

A 1995 report from the General Accounting Office (GAO) estimates that about 14 million students attend substandard schools, schools needing extensive repair or replacement. According to the GAO, "Most schools are unprepared for the 21st Century." They are talking about the physical buildings, not the curriculum. The report also noted that central cities schools with over 50 percent minority enrollment are more likely than others to have "unsatisfactory environmental conditions." There are plenty of research studies documenting the link between substandard facilities and poor academic performance. These children live in substandard buildings, attend substandard schools, and departments of education across the country insist that what we need to standardize is the curriculum we offer them. Politicians look at curriculum standards and offer congratulations on the educational equity achieved. There is a very real and very serious question to consider: How much academic success can our economy tolerate? Rather than spending so much of our time in battles of the phonics folk versus the literature lovers, maybe we should all take a look at the economic realities our students will face. These are the standards that matter. In *Created Unequal* (Free Press, 1998) James Galbraith deconstructs the notion that equalizing skills will equalize incomes. "It is one thing for a program to hold out, subsidize, and support new chances for individuals to compete on the educational and career ladders. It is something different to promise that the ladder itself will become shorter and wider as a result of an increase in the numbers crowding their way up the rungs. It is something entirely different to suppose that each new entrant and reentrant in the educational sweepstakes will enjoy a chance of success equally high as those who have already entered and won."

Galbraith says that the notion that education can cure the wage structure problem is a fantasy. It is, of course, a convenient fantasy for Standardistos to promote, another version of the Blame-the-Victim hypothesis. The workers are to blame, so the argument goes, because they lack the skills. Galbraith points out that such dangerous fantasies "insulate us from a serious discussion of why inequality has risen and what might be done about it."

Educational systems do not determine economic structures. Our economic structures are, of course, determined by "benefit to business," not by teacher intent, not even the intent of algebra teachers. What Galbraith calls the business world's "brutal skepticism" toward the nonutilitarian is painfully evident in the standards documents drafted by state boards of education. The city of Berlin spends more on the arts than does the U.S. government. France devotes vast expenditure on the arts, not because this has anything to do with GNP growth, but because French politicians believe that the public needs culture. But our leaders don't "get" it; instead, they threaten once again to abolish the meager support they give to culture.

In a nineties twist on Marie Antoinette's famous remark, "Let them eat cake," proponents of the special quarter-cent sales tax to build the Phoenix Diamondbacks a $355 million state-of-the-art baseball facility complete with a retractable roof and a swimming pool, pointed out, to those who spoke against taxing poor people to build such an edifice, that the baseball tax caused the price of an iced tall latte at Starbucks in Scottsdale to increase just one cent, from $2.40 to $2.41. In *Big League, Big Time*, Len Sherman chronicles the political standards that allowed the financial chicanery of raising $355 million for the stadium and another $130 million for the city's entrance fee to major league baseball. And there's more. The city of Phoenix condemned the property housing the Greyhound bus terminal so they could build a $43 million parking garage for the ballpark. That works out to $15,930 per space. Let the poor drink lattes and buy cars instead of riding the bus.

James Galbraith observes that those screaming the loudest to "end welfare as we know it" are precisely those who do not know it, those persons "detached from the life experiences of those on the receiving end." It is our strength as teachers that we are empathetic people; we try to walk in the shoes of our students. We must nurture this quality, fighting off all attempts of Standardisto baboons to strip it away. John Kenneth Galbraith once observed, "If all economists were laid end-to-end, it would be a good thing." That's an apt formula for Standardistos: end-to-end would be a good thing.

"Don't uses rotted names," warned the poet Wallace Stevens. Just because a word has five syllables doesn't mean it's worth anything. The great words of teaching are the one-syllable ones: read, write, teach, learn, work, skill, care, help, hope, trust, faith, love. And the greatest of these, of course, is love.

7

Counting on Kids and Their Teachers

WHO PUT EDUCATION WEEK IN CHARGE OF THE WORLD?

*P*eople who care about schools should keep a careful eye on what folks at *Education Week* are up to these days. In the name of excellence, or perhaps in the name of securing a big grant from the Pew Charitable Trusts, they seem to have elected themselves chief Standardistos of the land. In January 1997, I was surprised and disgruntled to receive a 238-page tome produced by *Education Week* titled *Quality Counts.* This so-called report on the condition of U.S. schools states its position as a mouthpiece for corporate America right up front. "As the new millennium approaches, there is growing concern that if public education doesn't soon improve one of two outcomes is almost inevitable:

- Our democratic system and our economic strength, both of which depend on an educated citizenry, will steadily erode; or,

- Alternative forms of education will emerge to replace public schools as we have known them."

Any time people start talking about the millennium, teachers had better duck. They're in for a barrage of easy denunciations of public schools. Conspiracy theorists please note the guest list at the corporate-politico-info-tainment education summit hosted by IBM: the Pew Charitable Trusts was represented (See Chapter Six). Funny thing: I thought *Education Week*'s function was to report the news, putting opinion on the back Commentary page. The report *Education Week* has produced isn't news, it's corporate cronyism; it offers not dispassionate reportage but deliberate deception, using statistics to tell any lie it damn well pleases.

People at *Education Week* seem to have elected themselves the *Consumer Reports* of public education, issuing scores on the teachers in every state. But they create categories that benefit neither teachers nor children; their categories march in lock-step behind the Education Summit called by President Clinton and Lou Gerstner. When we get the standards *Education Week* is calling for, the editors will be able to help the politicos issue these grades town by town, school corridor by school corridor. Without leaving Washington. These grades aren't based on kid-watching but on paper-piling.

January 1998 brought the second edition of *Quality Counts*, this one a 270-page tome with a tone similarly corporate-controlled. The son of *Quality Counts* opens with, "It's hard to exaggerate the education crisis in America's cities." The report goes on to talk of "islands of achievement" surrounded by "oceans of failure." Because the ideology is far more alarming than the rhetoric I will restrain myself—other than pointing out that the florid prose is the illegitimate progeny of *A Nation at Risk*.

In a category titled *Teachers Who Have the Knowledge Skills to Teach to Higher Standards*, the highest grade given in 1997 was an 84, which translates as a B on the *Education Week* scale. If I could only find some foundation funding, the Pew Charitable Trusts maybe, I'd love to spend a year deconstructing the linguistic hobbledehoy *Teachers Who Have the Knowledge Skills to Teach to Higher Standards*. And who's the smartest of them all? Sour grapes not being my style, I offer kudos to Kentucky, with the smartest teachers in the land in 1997.

In 1998, Oklahoma teachers were judged to be most knowledgeable, the most skilled to teach to higher standards. They received a 91, an A-. Minnesota teachers' skill level fell from B to C—in just one year; Vermont teachers fell from a B- to a C- in that same period, as did Georgia, among others. Iowa teachers, whose students' standardized test scores are among the top in the nation, rated a grade of C in 1997 and D+ in 1998. In 1997, three states ranked in the D range in terms of "teacher knowledge and skills to teach to higher standards"—Idaho, Arizona, and Hawaii; in 1998, 15 suffered this fate. Please excuse my repetition of the ungainly verbiage—teacher knowledge and skills to teach to higher standards. The words so boggle my mind that I feel the need to keep trying them out. The words do not flow easily off pen or tongue. Not to mention the underlying idea: The Pew Charitable Trusts and the folk at *Education Week* issue report cards on the teachers of America.

In addition to Iowa, South Carolina, Kansas, Rhode Island, Montana, Idaho, Alaska, Maine, New Hampshire, New Mexico, South Dakota, Nevada, Wyoming, Arizona, and Wisconsin suffer this ignominy of getting a D in teacher smarts. The latter two received grades of D-. Wisconsin is given the lowest rating in the nation—even though in the category of *States with significant urban centers, ranked by percent of students at NAEP "basic" level*, they are number one.

What's going on here? You look at how the states are ranked and you know there is something very peculiar about the definition of "teacher skill and knowledge." The first rule of journalism is operative here: *Education Week* publishes the report, and so *Education Week* gets to make the rules. It's freedom of the press to do what they damn well please.

Education Week has decided that twenty percent of the grade depends on whether the state provides time and money for professional development. Forty percent of the mark includes such criteria as:

- State has adopted standards for new teachers;

- State contributes to INTASC's development of new teacher assessments;

- State has established an independent professional standards board.

Certainly I am all in favor of states funding professional development, but to equate this with teachers savvy is worse than odd; it's malicious and underhanded and, well, it's loony. Have the graders at *Education Week* ever sat through a typical inservice presentation? Prize-winning science writer David Quammen says people who visit zoos are seeing "taxidermy on the hoof." Zoo visitors believe that the Bengal tiger (or the white rhino, or the giant panda, or the diademed sifaka) is alive and well because they have seen it. But, says Quammen, they haven't seen it. What they've seen are images, theatrical illusion. And theatrical illusion is just what hired-gun Standardistos at *Education Week* are getting from their numbers. To quote Quammen again, "Snow truths do exist but they're elusive and protean. Like snowflakes themselves, they tend to melt away when carried indoors." Snow truths are a nice metaphor for teaching truths because they immediately draw us to what we heard as children: No two snowflakes are alike. *Education Week* Standardistos need to take off their hubris cloaks and start looking at snowflakes.

We need only to read elsewhere in the booklet to find direct refutation of the grades handed out under the name of teacher knowledge and skills. Take Maine. Rated at the bottom of "teacher knowledge and skills," Maine is at the top of another chart titled *All Students Achieving at High Levels.* How did those Maine students score so well if their teachers are so incompetent? We can't make any judgments about Oklahoma as it did not participate in national assessments or data collection. Connecticut is the only state that scores high in both categories.

So Maine students tie for first place in the NAEP in math, and come out on top in science. But the quality of their teachers is rated as "D." Likewise, Montana teachers rate a D even though their students score among the top five states on NAEP. *Education Week* scorers rate Montana teachers so poorly because the state "still does not have any grade-by-grade benchmarks that spell out what students should know and be able to do." The fact that Montana students are achieving desired results without the benchmarks is irrelevant to the people who make the rules at *Education Week* whose unacknowledged mission is to support the goals of the corporate-politico-infotainment Standardistos. Follow the money: He who pays the piper gets to call the tune.

LET US COUNT THE FLEAS

Education Week's ratings of teachers would be shameful even if it made sense. But let's recognize this cur for what it is. This hound isn't just flea-ridden; this dog has mange. And I'd watch for frothing at the mouth.

This "Do it our way or else" jingoism comes right out of corporate America, behind the Goals 2000 juggernaut to produce national standards and tests for children and teachers. The pro-business skills rhetoric pretends that our nation lacks a sufficiently able work force. Teachers and students might be better served if *Education Week* took their Pew Charitable Funds windfall and investigated the numbers behind the claim that schools aren't producing enough skilled workers. There is plenty of evidence that we have a work force that is over-prepared for the jobs available (See Chapter Six).

I have had experience with *Education Week*'s "Do it our way or else" stance. I wrote a *Commentary* in which I paid tribute to what a black student taught me about how to teach remedial reading to seventh- and eighth-grade urban kids. Imagine my surprise upon reading my *Commentary* to see my black student had become transformed into a black teacher who acted as my mentor. In the standards-conscious halls of *Ed Week*, a teacher is supposed to teach her students, not learn from them.

Education Week identifies the Illinois English Language Arts Standards as the only state English language arts standards in the nation worthy of the grade of A. Illinois is the state that declares that "Research has identified exactly what reading skills a child needs" and that within five years "Every elementary school child will be able to read on grade level, with fluency and comprehension." Illinois reading standards are filled with verbs like *apply word analysis skills, comprehend, establish purposes, identify genres, check and clarify, summarize, analyze, make comparisons, identify*. I keep looking for *find joy in words*, but so far I haven't found it.

In Illinois, early elementary students are expected to: "Demonstrate focus, organization, elaboration and integration in written composition (e.g., short stories, letters, essays, reports)." And "Write letters, reports and stories based on acquired information." Pardon me? Early elementary as in grades one to three? This is why we now have second grade teachers in Illinois scrambling to push their kids into writing research reports. It sounds impressive, but I'd like to meet the early childhood specialist who would agree that it is educationally sound.

As such documents go, I will concede that the Illinois Standards could be worse. But these standards do not represent the best of what educators know about teaching language arts. I confess I just can't love a document that purports to be about improving the teaching and learning of reading and writing but fails to mention "reading for personal pleasure."

This is where all Standardistos miss the mark. Most of our students will not grow up to write short stories or research reports; they will not sit around discussing theme, plot, and setting after they read a book. But, if given a chance, even rotten readers, kids mainstreamed from special class, kids from one-parent families, kids on probation, bilingual, minimally brain-damaged, deaf, one-eyed kids will read willingly, even with enthusiasm. The sad thing is that schools rarely make the time to give kids the opportunity to prove this. I tell teachers that by February my third graders, sectioned off as the worst readers at that grade level, were moaning and groaning when I called a halt to sustained silent reading at the end of one hour each morning, and those teachers are amazed, shocked, and mystified. "When did you find time for skills?" they ask. Honest. It's the first question I'm always asked.

Leaving a child alone to savor a book, to get from it what he or she will, and then holding your tongue when the child closes the book, requires a tremendous act of faith—faith in children and faith in books. Sad to say, the Standardistos, the state school boards, the federalistos disbursing their Goals 2000 small change, the corporate and media watch dogs, are not amenable to acts of faith. They demand records: Competency checklists, scope and sequence charts, teachers marching in lockstep and parroting words handed out from the publishing conglomerates, national tests.

Trusting books, trusting children, trusting teachers, is revolutionary. Books are, after all, dangerous stuff. Leave a child alone with a book and you don't know what might happen. Leave a teacher alone with a room full of children and books and—well, it is the Standardistos' worst nightmare. For the politicos, the media pundits, and the professors who feel they must be in control, I commend Arnold Lobel's lovely little tale, "The Crocodile in the Bedroom," from *Fables* (Harper and Row, 1980). A crocodile who loved the neat and tidy rows of the flowers on the wallpaper in his bedroom was coaxed outside into the garden by his wife, who invited him to smell the roses and the lilies of the valley. "Great heavens!" cried the crocodile. "The flowers and leaves in this garden are growing in a terrible tangle! They are all scattered! They are messy and entwined!" Whereupon he went back to his room, seldom leaving his bed. He stared at the neat and tidy rows of flowers on the wallpaper and he turned a very pale and sickly shade of green. I would point out to standards enthusiasts that Lobel's moral, *Without a doubt, there is such a thing as too much order*, applies as much to classrooms as it does to wallpaper and real gardens.

Teachers are traditionally apolitical: Just let me shut the door and teach. These *Education Week* reports reveal that we can't dismiss Standardistos as far-right fundamentalist crackpots who probably aren't playing with a full deck. Instead, we must recognize that the Standardistos are well-organized, extremely savvy in manipulating the media, and they play with loaded dice. Teachers must realize that there is nobody out there protecting us.

A TEACHER'S WORKPLACE

I went to my first teaching job—in a Queens, New York, high school larger than my hometown—from an editorial job on Madison Avenue, and I was astonished that the teachers union contract stipulated that the Board of Education must supply an adequate amount of toilet paper. It seemed grossly unprofessional for a teachers union to be making toilet paper stipulations.

Then I moved to an urban school upstate, and I discovered what happens when union contracts don't order boards of education to provide such minimal standards for teachers' working conditions as an adequate supply of toilet paper. The calls for school standards never mention the quality of life, the basic human necessities, provided for the teachers and children in those schools.

In Queens, I shared the teacher desk with two other teachers; the teacher with most seniority got three drawers. Advocates for standards and excellence and all other good things should know that in most schools teachers don't have access to a phone, teachers don't have an office, and in some places they are lucky to have one drawer.

Teachers who take summer jobs in industry are astounded to discover that the coffee is free. In schools, nothing is free. Because of constant and continual shortages, teachers end up having to buy even the most basic of classroom supplies. One time I asked the school secretary for staples. "Put out your hand," she ordered and proceeded to count out seventeen staples into my outstretched palm. It is no wonder that teachers are notorious for stealing each other's supplies. That's why we write our names in huge indelible ink letters on every surface of everything we own. The kids don't want our ratty scissors, staplers, and tape dispensers, but our colleagues are desperate for those items. I have worked in schools where a chalkboard eraser was a carefully guarded item. I won't even go into the matter of adapter plugs.

When I taught in Queens, I couldn't stand the textbook, and so I needed lots of paper to reproduce better stories for the kids to read. I went in an hour early each morning so I could steal mimeo paper from the main office. Then they locked the supply cabinets, and I had to resort to buying a ream of my own. When I asked Patrick Shannon if I could take one of the titles he was considering for his own book, Pat reminded me that the first rule of teaching is to steal whatever you can. And yes, this book's title is his.

PRAYING FOR ABSENTEEISM

During that first year of teaching, the absentee list was circulated fourth period. We were supposed to compare the names of students absent from our classes with names on that official list and immediately report students who were cutting class. And so, every fourth period, I taught from the corner of the room near the doorway, watching for the hall monitor who distributed the absentee list. Cutters weren't my concern; I grabbed the list to see if by some miracle Eddie, the plague of not just my seventh-period class but of my life, was absent. For the first three periods each day I could nourish the hope that maybe Eddie hadn't showed up, that he wasn't even in the building. Then came the reality of fourth period. His name was never there. I didn't know it at the time but one of the great tenets underlying education-in-practice is that the hyperactive kid is never absent.

A few years later I taught in a tough school that bused kids home for lunch because members of the board of education insisted they did not want to institute a federal school lunch program that would subvert "every mother's privilege of feeding lunch to her children." To accommodate the buses going back and forth, our lunch break was one and a half hours long. One day a young substitute teacher, filling in for the seventh-grade math teacher, left for lunch, and he never came back. Since we were a downtown school, located only a block from the nearest bar, we figured if the principal really wanted to find this fellow, he wouldn't have far to look. But we also figured that, after an hour and a half of thinking about returning, he might be under the bar. We veterans hooted and hollered about this overwhelmed greenhorn, but my laughter was subdued. I wasn't so far from my Queens beginnings not to know just how that poor fellow felt. Writing in *Turning Stones* (Harcourt Brace, 1996), his account of working as a child welfare caseworker in New York City, Marc Parent says a favorite tenet of the office is "If ya ain't scared, ya ain't working." I'd subscribe to that for teaching, too. To be a good teacher is to know that at any moment you could get a pie in the face—or fall on your face.

Eddie, my ninth-grade student in Queens, was a non-reader. This much bandied-about term is one I use very carefully. As a medieval lit-major-cum-teacher with a skin-of-my-teeth emergency credential that put me in charge of one hundred and thirty-two students, it took me several months to figure out that this obnoxious brat of a boy, the terror of my days, couldn't read. And then, as green as I was, I took the Standardisto point of view: I found it amazing and appalling that a school system could allow a kid (with perfect attendance) to reach ninth grade without being able to read. Even as I was expressing outrage, I did remember one of own my high school classmates who couldn't read but who nonetheless received an athletic scholarship to Stanford. So much for standards.

At the end of that first semester I used the only weapon I knew about. I didn't just fail Eddie; I put a "personal conduct" demerit on his report card. A student couldn't graduate with this taint on his permanent record, and the mark could be erased only by "public service."

Real life is always stranger than fiction. That's why, when, at the end of that first semester Eddie appeared in my doorway after school and asked to earn public service credit by being my classroom aide for the second semester, I accepted him. At the time, I wondered if I'd lost my mind. Years later, I came to see that this was one of those teacherly moments, those moments when a teacher discovers who she is and in the process discovers a piece of what matters. Today, I am proud that as green as I was, when confronted by a kid I loathed and feared, I behaved well. I guess my acceptance of Eddie was a schoolhouse version of the definition of home: *The place where, when you knock on the door, they have to let you in.* A large number of us teachers choose to offer not justice, not standards, but compassion. So the monstrous kid to whom I'd given the conduct demerit the first semester worked it off the second semester.

Eddie was a terrific aide. He kept my waste cans emptied and stapled all my papers. Mostly he stood at my elbow, offering a running commentary on how a green teacher should deal with kids who didn't toe the line. Unfortunately, my virtue in granting Eddie this chance for atonement was not rewarded. Eddie was assigned to my English class that second semester. So he appeared in my second period class as exemplary civil servant and then reappeared fourth period as the hell raiser. Eddie and I both kept his two roles separate. I never berated the civil servant, and he never stopped being the terror of fourth period.

There is no question that I failed as Eddie's teacher. No matter what other fine acts I may perform as a teacher, I have to look back to Eddie with real regret, knowing he deserved better. But if he didn't learn from me, I did learn from him. For one thing, I learned that the student a teacher sees is far from being the whole child. Eddie the nonreader might have been a real snot, but Eddie the aide was an endearing little kid with a kind of screwball wisdom about how school was 'spozed to be—for other kids. Eddie the aide was always advising me that I was too easy on rotten kids like him.

Of course I wish I'd been able to teach Eddie to read. I blame my greenness for not even knowing how to try. I don't see that the Standardisto pronouncements would have helped. People who can prepare documents that declare "A commitment and plan of action is established to ensure that all students read and write at grade level" (California), and "students will perform above national averages on national measures of reading ability" (Illinois), are either crazy or crooked. In any case, they are operating in an academic twilight zone.

In bygone eras our society made room for these kids who weren't academically able but who could still be productive members of society. Today, the Standardistos are proclaiming, "Join the high-tech future, equipped with calculus, or you'll be nothing."

EDUCATIONAL GUIDE OR SQUADRON LEADER

Recently someone asked me why I didn't send Eddie to the office. The funny thing is that I didn't know a teacher could do that. I thought that being a teacher means you get shut up in a room with thirty kids, and you have to deal with whatever happens the best way you can. I did send a panicked message to my department chair the afternoon kids brought ice cream sandwiches from lunch and staged an ice cream war. But except for that one time, I didn't complain to anybody. I guess I didn't want to admit I couldn't do the job, but I really did accept it as something I had to cope with. And surviving that first year without sending kids to the office set a lifelong pattern. I'd done it once; I could do it again. A teacher takes the kids she's given, and she does the best she can. The saving grace is that "our best" does improve.

A clear benefit of not sending kids to the office *no matter what* is that a teacher who takes care of her own problems soon gains administrative kudos as a "good disciplinarian" and then is pretty much ignored. Teachers and principals develop an unofficial quid pro quo. I am sure I was allowed to get away with not using a basal because I showed up for hall duty on time and I "handled" difficult children without complaining.

One year a new, hot-shot supervisor in our district, a precursor of the Standardisto, was conducting official observations of reading lessons, treating teachers rather like assembly-line workers in a Swiss cuckoo clock factory. Teachers were "written up" if they weren't on the exact page in the text that their plans indicated they would be on. I regard ignoring lesson plans as a teacher's best opportunity for immediate gratification. I waited all year for this visit, wondering what would happen when the grand inquisitor of schedules didn't find me on a particular page in the text, because there were no texts.

Alas, it never happened. The grand inquisitor avoided my classroom, and at the end of the year my principal wrote up my official observation, saying he was "helping out." I'll never know for sure, but I think that principal decided to save my bacon, to make sure there was no conflict with the supervisor, no edict ordering me to use the basal. I had worked with that principal on and off over the years in three different schools, and we respected and even liked each other.

This was a principal who knew when and how to take risks. My second year of teaching seventh and eighth graders he let me scrap the remedial reading workbooks and kits and spend the whole budget on vouchers at a local bookstore: Once a month, kids went to the bookstore and chose their own books to read in the coming month. All the principal ever said to me was, "Sue, just pray the Board of Ed never gets wind of this—it would be both our necks." A principal who can take such a risk stands head and shoulders above a pack of Standardistos.

But in these days of rampaging Standardistos, an increasing number of principals are accepting the role of squadron leader. I know plenty of teachers who are openly envious when they hear I once had a principal who refused to speak to me for seven months. And when it happened to me, I knew to count my blessings.

BRIBES, LIES, AND MORE LIES

If state departments of education and local boards of education and teacher associations had any guts, they would have told the corporate-politico-infotainment league—the Standardistos, "We already have standards, thank you very much." But the federal politicos were offering bribes in the name of Goals 2000 to get everybody, but most particularly state departments of education, to pony up to the standards starting gate, and so a veritable stampede has resulted. The fact that standards ignore the needs of children and sell teachers short matters not. Operating on the premise that teachers will be forced to get in line once the national tests are in place, Standardistos move ahead with the education reform plans dreamed up in corporate boardrooms and conservative think tanks. This build-it-and-they-will-come theory may work for baseball stadiums, but real life isn't baseball, not yet anyway.

The standards of the late 1990s were spawned by *A Nation at Risk*, which appeared in 1983 and declared that our rotten schools produce a rotten workforce and hence we have failed in international competitiveness. With Standardistos screaming so loudly it's hard for the voice of reason to be heard. But here is an interestingly little fact: One hundred years ago, the high-school graduation rate was three percent; today it's 83 percent, 91 percent if you count GED recipients. Here are a few more statistics that we don't see making headlines. According to the UNESCO *Statistical Yearbook 1997*, here are the percentages of population with at least some high school: U.S. 91.3 percent Japan: 67.3 percent.

Few people seem interested in hearing that, internationally, American students place second in reading, and our top readers, those above the 90th percentile, are the best in the world. When Standardistos display their cooked data, just remember that the only thing we need to know about statistics is that the Hundred Years' War lasted 116 years. Most certainly, Eddie didn't belong in the traditional/standardisto high school intent on preparing students to be high tech employees. Eddie was a rotten student, but he was an excellent worker. Instead of decreeing he must take foreign language and algebra, why don't we sit down and talk about the fact that it is morally wrong and practically nonsensical to throw our Eddies away?

SETTING APOSTROPHE STANDARDS

The poet John Ciardi once pointed out that the U.S. Constitution gives every American the inalienable right to make a damn fool of himself. Nonetheless, it seems like there should be weight restrictions on the foolish documents Standardistos can send into our schools. We need a gatekeeper, someone who stamps items: "Return to sender. Exceeds allowable weight limitations."

The proliferation of standards documents results in the de-skilling and the deprofessionalizing of teachers. How else are teachers to feel except helpless in the face of being told to *deliver* a curriculum that is invented by external authorities? Nationwide, we have the lowest retention rate of teachers in history. This standards movement is being led by a monolithic big business whose focus is on the product rolling off the conveyor belt, or out of the sweatshops in Asia. To big business, students are merely employees-in-training, and employees are disposable, not worth as much attention as a gnat on a rhino's rear.

What few people acknowledge is that there is no "reform" in the Standardistos' documents: Standardistos are trying to pass off macaroni and cheese skills as *Ziti con Formaggio Velveta di Alfa Romeo* gourmet dining. They merely want to perpetuate the same old skill drill that kids have been resisting all this century. And, among others, they've fooled just about all the newspaper editors in the country. I would point out that finding a grammatical flaw in a stop sign is not a sign of academic excellence. I did, after all, live in Pennsylvania for a few years, where local grammar zealots saw the dissolution of western civilization embodied in license plates that declared, "You've Got a Friend in Pennsylvania."

When I taught third grade I was so overwhelmed by trying to immerse my students, who thought they hated reading, in books, I never had time for grammar. None. I took heart from Eudora Welty's reminiscence that "None of my teachers managed to scare me into grammar." I concentrated on reading aloud to the children, helping them learn to read silently to themselves, and exchanging letters every day. We read a lot and we wrote a lot. We wrote letters, thank you notes, get well cards, letters of advice, invitation, lists, menus, acrostics, tongue twisters, riddles, poems, tall tales, skits, personal narratives.

Now here's the part that will upset everybody, Standardistos and writing process people alike: I explained to my students what an editor does and told them that for a whole lot of their writing I would be their editor. Every day I gave them a writing topic—based on something happening in their lives, on a snippet from a favorite picture book, on a zany idea. Everybody wrote on the same topic and I typed them up in a small booklet, correcting spelling and such as I went. I did this because my goal was fluency and pleasure in words and because I wanted parents to take pleasure from the children's writing. When children hate literacy activities as much as these children did, a teacher must take desperate measures. Every night, the children took home a broadside to read to their families. Thus, every family was reading every child's words. When the children offered quite witty advice on how to get a hippopotamus stuck in the bathtub out, the custodian told me dads were reading the broadside aloud at the local bar.

In the spring these formerly rotten readers took the dreaded Stanford test in language arts, and the results were rather stunning. Most of the children scored on or near grade level in reading comprehension. Most of the children also scored above grade level in usage, punctuation, and spelling. All I could figure out was that, on standardized tests, usage, punctuation, and spelling are really proofreading—choose the right answer. I postulate that my students had read so much that they could recognize what "looked" right even if they didn't produce this correctness in their own writing.

Okay, I confess I probably skewed the results a bit. Right before we opened the sealed test I told my students I'd break the knuckles of anybody who chose an answer that added an apostrophe to a passage. "We do not do apostrophes in this room," I announced in my sternest voice, the same kind of voice my father used to tell me not to get out of the car. That was a lucky guess on my part. Two items gave kids the choice of adding apostrophes (and anybody who knows third graders knows how prone they are to pepper their papers with extra apostrophes—if you allow the critters into the classroom), and two items on one section of the Stanford really affect the score. We will avert a lot of agony if we banned apostrophe use until age sixteen. After all, most apostrophe errors are sins of commission, not omission. If you ban the beasties from your classroom, you find you hardly miss them. I would only add that what was good enough for Emily Dickinson is plenty good enough for me. Emily did not use the apostrophe.

BEWILDERED SOMETIMES

When Daniel Boone was in his eighties, he was asked if he'd ever been lost. Boone replied that no, he was never lost, but, he admitted, "I was bewildered once for three days." Any teacher who isn't bewildered about three days a week isn't worth her salt. Bewildering as it may be, I know that my students learned more from my getting them to watch for the first asparagus ads in the newspaper each spring, from my devotion to letter writing, from my love of knock-knock jokes and hink pinks, from seeing me reading a novel during silent reading, from my use of a fountain pen, and from my countless personality quirks, than from anything in the guides sent out occasionally from the state department of education.

The California *Field Review of the Draft Reading/Language Arts Curriculum Framework, K–12* spells out in painful detail the "Instructional Delivery" (there go those educational terminologists again) for teaching fourth graders to revise "Self-Written Compositions."

1. Define deletion and tell why it is important to know when and how to delete information from writing.

2. Establish a rule for determing if information should be deleted.

3. Present the four steps in deleting and revising. (Steps given.)

4. Model multiple paragraphs containing information that needs to be deleted. The text should include only words that students can identify and vocabulary for which they know the meanings. Ensure the information to delete represents the parts of speech (e.g., adjectives, verbs).

5. Encourage students to think out loud as they read the paragraph and: 1) locate the sentences/phrases/words that do not tell more about the topic and 2) use the proofreader's deletion mark to eliminate words to delete.

6. Repeat this on a few examples.

They call this "Instructional Delivery"; we used to call it workbooks, and now, knowing what we do about how children learn to write, we can only call it lunacy. Number four offers piquant possibility— some textual information *not* representing the parts of speech. And of course the Standardistos are right: If you've got non-parts of speech in your paragraph, you'd better remove them at once.

I have plenty of firsthand classroom evidence that when children write daily letters, when they use wonderful snippets from literature to inform their own writing, their writing improves. I'd like to see research evidence that supports this Standardisto notion that doing workbook exercises on other peoples' bad writing ever improved a fourth grader's prose.

The Standardisto obsession with control is evidenced in their insistence that kids get only text for which they can identify all the words. If words don't amaze and astound readers, what's the point? When Beatrix Potter's editor complained about her use of *soporific* in the opening to *The Tale of the Flopsy Bunnies.* Potter replied, "Children like a fine word occasionally."

When Chris encountered "soporific," he was astounded. He'd already read at least half a dozen of the little Potter books and hadn't encountered anything like this word before. "Look at this word!" he exclaimed. I told him what it meant. And showed him there were context clues, those things frowned on and even forbidden by Standardistos in California. I didn't even make Chris enter the word in his vocabulary journal but let him just sit there trying it out on his tongue. I didn't worry about whether other children in the room would or would not be entranced by "soporific," because I know that when you believe in books and in students, students—one by one—encounter wonderful words, words that knock their socks off. They do it all time. They just don't do it on schedule.

The above Instructional Delivery system sets us back at least three decades in helping children become better writers. I want to see us stop using the writing process in some sort of regime of knee-jerk automaticity, not abandon it for the skill-drill ritual of practice, practice, practice on deleting information that "represents the parts of speech" in other peoples' writing. Correcting other peoples' writing is a valuable skill if you grow up to be an editor; it is not writing.

Practice, practice, practice is, of course, the Standardistos' anthem. The curriculum terminologists who wrote this document say that "Advanced Learners" may not require as much practice as their peers. "Low-performing students may require," you guessed it, more practice. Standardistos believe that instructional delivery consists of practice that is "frequent enough to provide for understanding and retention." They provide advice not only for the instructional deliverer but also for the publisher: "Publishers will always be safe in providing more resources for a given set of standards . . . than one might think sufficient for average students." Thicker workbooks?

"Control" is the issue throughout this and other Standardisto documents: The state of California is in control of the standards, the curriculum, the workbooks, and the instructional deliverers, and those instructional deliverers are in charge of the kids.

IT'S STILL THE ECONOMY, STUPID

On *60 Minutes*, Lesley Stahl interviewed a man who had a website on which he posted hundreds of pages about the crash of TWA Flight 800. He was describing these pages when Stahl interrupted, "Excuse me, but it looks like you have made up all this information. You don't have any research to back it up. This may be malicious speculation." The man replied, "So? If people don't like this website, then can go to another website." I guess this is the Cyberspace version of *Let them eat cake*, or *When the Chicago schools don't have the money to open, let the kids move to another city*. Such snollygostianism seems well on its way to being a national credo: You can make up anything you want to—and let the buyer/viewer/learner beware. But when we accept this as a national credo, who will protect the children?

Calvin Trillin once said that of course he made up the statistics in his book, noting that at the price you paid for the book you can't expect genuine statistics. But he was kidding. Wall Street speculators and Standardistos are dead serious with their use of phony figures.

In 1992, when E. Gerald Corrigan was president of the Federal Reserve Bank of New York, he warned that overexposure to derivatives could throw the U.S. financial system into crisis. But by 1994, he had been hired by Goldman, Sachs and was discounting his own warnings. Frank Partnoy reports in *F.I.A.S.C.O.* that Morgan Stanley's president John Mack was typical of the mercenaries who loved derivatives. Soon after the first big corporate losses were announced, Mack told a group of managing directors, "There's blood in the water. Let's go kill someone." In December 1994, Orange County California filed the largest municipal bankruptcy petition in history. The losses included the monies of two hundred schools, cities, and special districts, and amounted to nearly $1,000 for every man, woman, and child in the county. This came less than four months after Moody's Investor Service, the most sophisticated of ratings agencies, had given Orange County's debt an A1 rating and had stated in a cover memo, "Well done, Orange County."

As it is wont to do, Congress held hearings about regulating derivatives. All attempts to set some standards for financial wheeling and dealing failed. Partnoy observes that in the two election cycles previous to these legislation attempts legislators had received $100 million in contributions from banks, investment firms, and insurance companies. I'm sure that was just a coincidence.

The state of California also held regulatory hearings. In the face of the disaster in Orange County, they ended up passing some laws; they passed laws regulating the way California teachers teach spelling.

Nearly three decades ago, Neil Postman and Charles Weingartner aptly observed that because of the nature of the schools, anyone teaching for change has to see teaching as a subversive activity. As any veteran teacher knows, it's easier to move a graveyard than to make substantive change in a district curriculum. The amazing thing about the current standards swamping schools is that a whole lot of the items look very familiar. I mean, what did the Standardisto come up with in the California history standards? California missions in fourth grade, Egyptians in sixth. I'd guess that most of America has studied the Egyptians in sixth for most of this century, and probably it is not a bad thing. So why all the fuss? Egyptians in sixth grade represents just about two minutes of the Standardisto curriculum day. There is plenty of reason for the fuss; the fuss just needs to get a whole lot louder.

A provocative point to consider is that both Theodore Sizer and E.D. Hirsch, Jr., are against Standards. Appearing on National Public Radio, Sizer and Hirsch voiced disagreement about many things, but they agree on a very fundamental issue. They both say standards imposed by an outside entity are a very bad idea. Hirsch says it's fine if people want to choose his core knowledge program as their standards, but that choice must be made "at the building level." Sizer says that national standards are "a terrifying idea." Sizer advocates focusing on a few really powerful ideas—"and I don't want someone far from my school to pick those ideas." Sizer says that smart people at the school level must find out what kids know and "teach them from there." Sizer also observes, "You can't teach kids well if you don't know them well."

Sizer speaks of the need for strong habits of mind rather than "sweeping coverage of facts which are whisked by students and quickly forgotten." Hirsch defends a shared body of knowledge that first graders learn, a shared body of knowledge that second graders learn, insisting that "education is cumulative" and that if you start early enough "you can bring all children up to a very high level." Hirsch says that when you hear the term "developmentally appropriate," you should check your wallet. He claims there is no scientific basis for its use and that it is used only to hold children back. Hirsch, of course, has a cheap, $10.95 (in paperback) per teacher capita solution: Just give every teacher a copy of *What Your Kindergartner Needs to Know, What your 1st Grader Needs to Know*, ad infinitum/nauseum.

A DIRTY LITTLE SECRET

Although most teachers avoid talking about it, the savviest among us are privy to a dirty little secret. I feel free to reveal it because corporate America won't have a clue as to what I am talking about. Are you ready? The fact is that kids don't necessarily learn what teachers teach. Before I got middle-aged and stodgy, I would have left out the "necessarily" in that statement. Because classroom stories both inform and illuminate my life, I offer a story.

One year in the bleak upstate New York November of my life, I became determined to teach something. I decided to teach a concrete, observable, testable fragment of information. I decided that my seventh and eighth graders should "exhibit understanding" of some geographical features. God knows why, but I began to drill them on the names of cities, states, rivers, and lakes. I know there are plenty of Standardistos out there who won't be able to grasp this, but for poor, urban kids—kids who never take a drive around the block in a family car, never mind a cross-country trek—these geographical notions are a mystery.

First, we had a quiz on all of this stuff once a week. Then, as the weeks rolled by and the failing quizzes piled up, I got desperate and began testing every day. I mean, this was a gambit I wanted to win. At that particular time in my career, it was important to me to know that I was transmitting some bit of information to students; I guess I needed to prove that I could write a message on John Locke's blank slate. The test was the same every day: Name three countries. Name three states. Name three rivers. To understand the surreal quality of all this, you should know that our school was located about five blocks from the Hudson River. My students could warn me about not eating no rank fish caught from the polluted Hudson, but ask them to "Name a river" and they drew a blank. These were seventh and eighth graders. Go back to Chapter Five and take a look at what California Standardistos decree seventh and eighth graders will learn.

The kids proved me a failure. They never did pass that geography quiz. But in January, on the first day back from Christmas vacation, 62 percent of my students showed up waving fountain pens, their Christmas gift of choice, as they informed me. Can you imagine urban ghetto kids showing up at school waving fountain pens? Are you surprised? Confused? Guess what. Those obstreperous seventh and eighth graders didn't give a fig for their teacher's curriculum agenda, but they were fascinated by the fact that she wrote with a fountain pen.

I know there is a deep moral in this story. For starters, it undoubtedly pushes a pie in the face of Standardistos, but I prefer to leave it "as is," a glorious tribute to the magic and mystery of teaching. And learning. The best thing we teachers have to take to our students is ourselves, who we are as people. This is what is so scary about teaching. We don't teach standards, not even international world-class standards; the best we have to take to our students looks back at us from the mirror every morning.

There isn't anything crucial for elementary school kids to know: Not igneous rocks, not Egyptians, not Iroquois, not Washington's battle plan, not apostrophes. By the end of eighth grade a kid needs to be able to read with understanding and pleasure and have some notion of how our number system works. But these basic needs are subverted by the Standardisto pronouncements that kids must learn Iroquois and igneous, or whatever. As I've already confessed, I have drifted in and out of becoming obsessed with teaching something. In moments of desperation I have even tried to teach Iroquois and apostrophes. And when the kids didn't learn it, I became the injured party, victimized by them crazy kids. But then I was fortunate enough to be visited by those flashes of insight that come from close classroom observation, the kind of insight you couldn't deliver to a Standardisto with a sledgehammer. Or an unabridged dictionary. Close classroom encounters convince me that it's the textbooks and the scope and sequence charts and the spic-and-span skills—all the accouterments of "standards"—that are crazy, not the kids.

We need to remind ourselves that the California State Board of Education reveals its purpose in the first paragraph of the preface to the Reading/Language Arts Curriculum Framework, issued June 12, 1998: "In order for high school graduates in California to proceed to higher education institutions or to be employable and meet the unprecedented economic and technological challenges of the 21st Century, they must. . . ." And so, in the name of the Fortune 500, Standardistos deliver a swarm of standards that have everything to do with discrete bits of information that aren't going to "stick" to this generation of learners any better than they did for my generation. Because the facts we teach are so ephemeral and so fleeting, because our society is increasingly out of joint, it is crucial that we ignore the content standards and continue to nurture the children in our care.

Houston professor Barbara Foorman insists that, when Standardistos take over, we can be relieved that "variability is eliminated." Others disagree. As eighty-seven-year-old Robert Frost remarked in a letter to his friend, the poet Louis Untermeyer, "in art, as in nature, we want all the differences we can get. In society too." I would add, "and especially in classrooms."

Mostly we teachers are secretive about what we really do. Tired of being pursued like horse thieves, tired of being blamed for society's ills, we circle the wagons and take cover rather than speak out about how meaningless the standards are. That masterly and subtle teacher and writer Philip Lopate once observed that "the art of teaching is knowing when a student is best left alone and when he is ripe to receive your help." Lopate adds, "the moment of ripeness is different in each student."

If a teacher could keep a detailed diary of her day, with a minute-by-minute account of what she does, Standardistos would be dumbfounded. Yes, there are those delicious moments of student ripeness, but the in-between times, the times when students are very reluctant to receive our help, are often eternal, defying any Standardisto notion of efficient delivery systems in the classroom. Jack set the "ripening" record in my teaching career, sitting in a corner by himself playing Scrabble for six months. And to confuse Standaristos further, Jack represents one of my teaching triumphs.

But the born-again Standardistos are in hot pursuit of streamlined students. When asked on the Albany, New York, public radio station, WAMC, "What about kids who fail the Regents?" New York State Education Commissioner Richard Mills says, "They can take the exam three times. There's plenty of time before twelfth grade to master this material. We've sent sample exams to teachers, we've put sample items on the web page, we've put out a reading list. We are not going to back away from the standards. Kids face another test later on—that job interview. It's so much smarter now to say, 'Here's what you need to know' than to have them fail later. This is our message: This is the standard you must meet."

Mills says, "I am responsible for making sure student performance improves in the Regents tests. This is a hard job, but it's fair. I know what I have to do. I'm making sure New York State students know what they have to do."

It sounds noble, but veteran New York teachers say that if all students must pass Regents exams to get a high school diploma, the only solution will be to make the Regents tests easier—rather ironic, in the name of standards, to simplify New York's premier set of tests. Who put New York Regents test writers in charge of the universe? How do they know what kids "need to know"—in job interviews—or real life? What *is* the test for life, anyway?

Whatever it is, I doubt that it is machine-scorable. Even worse is the demeaning, deskilling notion of Mills' argument: That high schoolers not traditionally successful in school will have a curriculum that consists of three years of trying to pass a test.

What worries me is that the Standardisto requirements are accepted as a given; there is no talk of what good these requirements do for students. I think of a line in Amanda Cross's *An Imperfect Spy* (Ballentine Books, 1996): "It comes over me in waves that sitting around discussing *Middlemarch*—which Virginia Woolf called the last novel written for adults—is not going to lead them [graduate students] or me to any common ground." We hear lots of talk of world–class standards leading students into world–class jobs with world–class paychecks, but there is no talk of our improved education system educating citizens for the common ground of a democracy, no talk of the standards that will help our children build better lives, build a better world. Remember, the history standards in California were introduced with the exultation that such standards would prepare students to fight for their country.

I find it kind of heartwarming to hear about some senators going to read with children in Washington, D.C. schools, but when political leaders declare that the presence of volunteer reading tutors in crumbling schools, schools without the services of professional librarians or well-stocked libraries, will transform every third grader in the land into an independent reader, they are merely spewing forth phantasmic puffery. Of more significance is the proposed legislation of California Congresswoman Zoe Lofgren, who proposes giving federal monies to states willing to reorganize the starting times of their high schools. Lofgren points to studies showing that the majority of adolescents need to sleep later in the day than most school starting times permit. And there's another benefit besides student contentment: Start schools later and they get out later, thus eliminating the problem of unsupervised juveniles running amok on city streets at three o'clock in the afternoon. Clearly, if high school schedules followed the dictates of adolescent psychology/physiology rather than the dictates of the bus schedulers, everybody would benefit. It is too obvious and simple an idea to go anywhere. And by the fall of 1998, even Lofgren wasn't pushing it. Like her colleagues in Congress, she was more interested in sex than school schedules. Her website invited visitors to "Read my Floor Speech on the Starr Report." But she had the glimmer of a good idea, and just in case the Starr Report goes away in our lifetime, and just in case Lofgren gets reelected, here is her web address: http://www.house.gov/lofgren.

What we need to do is pressure our Congress persons to do more. Instead of fooling around with national tests or bribing states into establishing state tests, we should ask the federal government for help in setting miminum standards for making sure the nation's children are cared for. We could turn our schools into places that truly serve children. Keep schools open twenty-four hours a day, serving three meals a day (plus snacks) to children, providing medical services, psychological services, and whatever else the children need.

IF YOU'RE SURE YOU KNOW THE SOLUTION, YOU ARE PART OF THE PROBLEM

I'd like to close by repeating a couple of penultimate Standardisto pronouncements:

- Every elementary school child will be able to read on grade level, with fluency and comprehension.

- Every elementary school teacher will be able to teach reading using comprehensive, research-based methods.

These statements come from the Illinois State Board of Education, but they are so generalized in their arrogance that they could be from almost any state document of empty claims. The language arts standards of my former school district look as though they were copied out of a table of contents of a textbook, and not an innovative textbook at that. This document declares, "The standards apply to all students regardless of their experiential background, capabilities, developmental and learning differences, interests or ambitions." Indeed. These Standardisto statements prove a major tenet of education: If you're sure you know the solution, you are part of the problem.

We should adopt the mountain-climbing philosophy of reading: How you get to the top is as important as getting there. The second grader who reads on grade level after reading books like *Frog and Toad* is a very different reader from the on-grade-level reader who has had a year of mastering consonant blends.

Helping students acquire skills that will enable them to be productive members of tomorrow's workforce should be only one very small mission of our schools. More importantly, we need to help students acquire the habits of mind to become good human beings: good parents, good friends, and good citizens of our democracy. We need to help students learn to care about themselves, to care about one another, and to care also about people they've never met. In *Letters from the Country* (Penguin, 1982), a book every Standardisto should read but, lacking that, everyone else must read, Carol Bly urges small towns to confer their own "Nobel prizes" on the men and women they feel have made the greatest contributions to the human family. Would anyone beyond the city limits pay attention to the results? Let's teach kids that it doesn't matter, and help them see that human values cannot be the result of taking a poll.

Finding out what does matter is crucial. In *The Spirit Catches You and You Fall Down: A Hmong Child, Her American Doctors, and the Collision of Two Cultures* (Farrar Straus Giroux, 1997), Anne Fadiman observes that the Hmong are routinely called this country's least successful refugees. They flunk the standard American test of success, which is, of course, economic. But if one applies social indices to the Hmong's life in the United States, they score better than most Americans. In rates of crime, child abuse, illegitimacy, and divorce, the Hmong come out on top. We should look at the Hmong and ask ourselves just how we want to measure success.

What confuses the Standardistos is the fact that the map is *not* the territory. Their documents are not the classrooms. As it happens, their documents aren't even *about* classrooms. In a deep sense, that's okay. After all, *Walden* isn't about the woods or *Desert Solitaire* about the desert. What those books are really about are living alone, living with purpose and honor. In a deep sense, the Standardisto documents are not about curriculum; they are about bureaucracy, group-think, and getting control of other people.

America's teachers and children don't need national committees to grade their worth. We need local teachers to reflect on their own experiences, to figure out how the students, the curriculum, and even the bureaucracy interact in a process we call education. The essence of being a teacher is knowing who you are, where you are—and liking what you find. Being a teacher means being able to draw your own map—instead of relying on mass-produced tourist guides. Being a teacher means understanding that the best map you draw still is *not* the territory.

The poet W. S. Merwin observed that "Any work of art makes one very simple demand on anyone who genuinely wants to get in touch with it. And that is to stop. You've got to stop what you're doing, what you're thinking, and what you're expecting and just be there for the poem for however long it takes." I don't know that I have ever read a better description of what it means to be a teacher. To be a teacher, you've got to stop your frantic busy-ness, stop what you're doing, stop looking for what you're looking, stop expecting what you're expecting, stop promising to deliver the Standardisto product on schedule. Stop, and just be there for the child—for however long it takes. Stop is a good word for teachers. It is a very good word for a teacher to take to heart. Stop.

Bibliography

Apple, Max. *Free Agents*, Harper and Row, 1984.

Berliner, David, and Bruce Biddle. *The Manufactured Crisis: Myths, Fraud, and the Attack on America's Public Schools*, Addison Wesley, 1995.

Bly, Carol. *Letters from the Country*, Penguin, 1982.

Boutwell, Clinton. *Shell Game: Corporate America's Agenda for Schools*, Phi Delta Kappa, 1997.

Bracey Gerald. "The Truth About America's Schools: The Bracey Reports 1991–1998", *Phi Delta Kappa*, 1997.

Bray, Rosemary. *Unafraid of the Dark*, Random House, 1998.

Children's Defense Fund. *The State of America's Children*, Beacon Press, 1998.

Cross, Amanda. *An Imperfect Spy*, Ballantine Books, 1986.

Csikszentimihaly, Mihaly. *Talented Teenagers: The Roots of Success and Failure*, Cambridge University Press, 1993.

Davis, Mike. *The Ecology of Fear*, Henry Holt, 1998.

Diegmueller, Karen, and Debra Viadero, "Playing Games with History", *Education Week*, Nov. 15, 1995.

Diller, Lawrence. *Running on Ritalin*, Bantam, 1998.

Education Week. *Quality Counts*, 1997.

Education Week. *Qualtiy Counts*, 1998.

Fadiman, Anne. *The Spirit Catches You and You Fall Down*, Farrar, Straus Giroux, 1997.

Galbraith, James. *Created Unequal*, Free Press, 1998.

Gerstner, Louis V. with Rodger D. Semerad, Denis Philip Doyle, William B. Johnston. *Reinventing Education*, Dutton, 1994.

Gordon, Suzanne. *Life Support*, Little, Brown, 1997.

Hawkins, David. *The Informed Vision*, Agathon/Schocken, 1974.

Hirsch, E. D. Jr. *Cultural Literacy*, Houghton Mifflin, 1987.

Humphreys, Josephine. *Fireman's Fair*, Penguin, 1992.

Illinois State Board of Education. *The Little Red Reading Book*, 1997.

Kearns, David T. *Winning the Brain Race*, Institute for Contemporary Studies, 1991.

Kohn, Alfie. "Only For My Kid: How Privileged Parents Undermine School Reform", *Phi Delta Kappa*, April, 1998.

Kohn, Alfie. *Punished By Rewards*, Houghton Mifflin, 1995.

Kohn, Alfie. *Beyond Discipline*, Association for Supervision and Curriculum Development, 1996.

Kozol, Jonathan. *Savage Inequalities*, Crown, 1991.

Krashen, Stephen. *Every Person A Reader: An Alternative to the California Task Force Report on Reading*, Heinemann, 1996.

Lobel, Arnold. *Fables*, Harper and Row, 1980.

Mathews, Jay. *Class Struggle*, Times Books, 1998.

Matthews, Anne. *Bright College Years*, Simon & Schuster, 1997.

Naipaul, Shiva. *An Unfinished Journey*, Viking Press, 1987.

National Council of Teachers of English/International Reading Association. *Standards for the English Language Arts*, 1996.

Ohanian, Susan. "Finding a 'Loony List' While Searching for Literacy", *Education Week*, May 6, 1987.

Ohanian, Susan. *Garbage Pizza, Patchwork Quilts, and Math Magic*, W. H. Freeman, 1992.

Ohanian, Susan. "A Not-So-Tearful Farewell to William Bennett", *Phi Delta Kappan*, September, 1988.

Oakes, Jeannie. *Keeping Track*, Yale University Press, 1996.

Parent, Mark. *Turning Stones*, Harcourt Brace, 1996.

Parrish, Peggy. *Teach Us, Amelia Bedelia*, Greenwillow,1980.

Partnoy, Frank. *F.I.A.S.C.O.*, Norton, 1997.

Paterson, Katherine. *The Spying Heart*, Dutton, 1989.

Potter, Beatrix. *The Tale of the Flopsy Bunnies*, Frederick Warne, 1909.

Proctor, Robert. *Cancer Wars*, Basic Books, 1995.

Quindlen, Anna. *How Reading Changed My Life*, Ballantine, 1998.

Reif, Linda. *Seeking Diversity*, Heinemann, 1997.

Scholes, Robert. *The Rise and Fall of English*, Yale, 1998.

Schrag, Peter, and Diane Divoky. *The Myth of the Hyperactive Child*, Dell, 1975.

Scleszka, Jon. *Squids Will Be Squids*, Viking, 1998.

Seuss, Dr. *Hop on Pop*, Random House, 1963.

Sherman, Len. *Big League, Big Time*, Pocket, 1998.

Simmons, Deborah C. and Edward J. Kaméenui. *Draft Reading/Language Arts Curriculum Framework, K-12*, California Department of Education, 1998.

Sobel, Dava. *Longitude*, Walker, 1995.

Suskind, Ron. *A Hope in the Unseen*, Broadway, 1998.

Taylor, Denny. *Beginning to Read and The Spin Doctors of Science*, NCTE, 1998.

Thornton, Tamara Plakins. *Handwriting in America*, Yale University Press, 1996.

Toch, Thomas. *In the Name of Excellence*, Oxford University Press, 1991.

Wilkinson, Todd. *Science Under Siege*, Johnson Books, 1998.